00 0088 741

STUDY GUIDES

(

**This book is to be returned on or before
the last date stamped below.**

Macmillan Study Guides

A Handbook of Writing for Engineers *Joan van Emden*
Effective Communication for Science and Technology *Joan van Emden*
Key Concepts in Politics *Andrew Heywood*
Linguistic Terms and Concepts *Geoffrey Finch*
Literary Terms and Criticism (second edition) *John Peck and
 Martin Coyle*
The Mature Student's Guide to Writing *Jean Rose*
Practical Criticism *John Peck and Martin Coyle*
The Student's Guide to Writing *John Peck and Martin Coyle*
The Study Skills Handbook *Stella Cottrell*
Studying Economics *Brian Atkinson and Susan Johns*
Studying History (second edition) *Jeremy Black and Donald M. MacRaild*

How to Begin Studying English Literature (second edition)
 Nicholas Marsh
How to Study a Jane Austen Novel (second edition) *Vivien Jones*
How to Study Chaucer (second edition) *Rob Pope*
How to Study Foreign Languages *Marilyn Lewis*
How to Study an E. M. Forster Novel *Nigel Messenger*
How to Study a Thomas Hardy Novel *John Peck*
How to Study James Joyce *John Blades*
How to Study Linguistics *Geoffrey Finch*
How to Study Modern Poetry *Tony Curtis*
How to Study a Novel (second edition) *John Peck*
How to Study a Poet (second edition) *John Peck*
How to Study a Renaissance Play *Chris Coles*
How to Study Romantic Poetry (second edition) *Paul O'Flinn*
How to Study a Shakespeare Play (second edition) *John Peck and
 Martin Coyle*
How to Study Television *Keith Selby and Ron Cowdery*

HOW TO STUDY
JAMES JOYCE

John Blades

© John Blades 1996

Published by
MACMILLAN PRESS LTD
Houndmills, Basingstoke, Hampshire RG21 6XS
and London
Companies and representatives
throughout the world

ISBN 0–333–59205–0

This book is printed on paper suitable for recycling and
made from fully managed and sustained forest sources.

A catalogue record for this book is available
from the British Library.

10 9 8 7 6 5 4 3
11 10 09 08 07 06 05 04

Printed in China

Contents

For Elaine

General editors' preface

Everybody who studies literature, either for an examination or simply for pleasure, experiences the same problem: how to understand and respond to the text. As every student of literature knows, it is perfectly possible to read a book over and over again and yet still feel baffled and at a loss as to what to say about it. One answer to this problem, of course, is to accept someone else's view of the text, but how much more rewarding it would be if you could work out your own critical response to any book you choose or are required to study.

The aim of this series is to help you develop your critical skills by offering practical advice about how to read, understand and analyse literature. Each volume provides you with a clear method of study so that you can see how to set about tackling texts on your own. While the authors of each volume approach the problem in a different way, every book in the series attempts to provide you with some broad ideas about the kinds of texts you are likely to be studying, and some broad ideas about how to think about literature; each volume then shows you how to apply these ideas in a way which should help you construct your own analysis and interpretation. Unlike most critical books, therefore, the books in this series do not simply convey someone else's thinking about a text, but encourage you and show you how to think about a text for yourself.

Each book is written with an awareness that you are likely to be preparing for an examination, and therefore practical advice is given not only on how to understand and analyse literature, but also on how to organise a written response. Our hope is that although these books are intended to serve a practical purpose, they may also enrich your enjoyment of literature by making you a more confident reader, alert to the interest and pleasure to be derived from literary texts.

John Peck
Martin Coyle

Acknowledgements

The author and publishers wish to thank the following for permission to use copyright material:

the Estate of James Joyce for extracts from *A Portrait of the Artist as a Young Man*, *Stephen Hero*, *Ulysses*, *Finnegans Wake* and the stories in *Dubliners* by James Joyce; copyright © the Estate of James Joyce.

Every effort has been made to trace all the copyright holders but if any have been inadvertently overlooked the publishers will be pleased to make the necessary arrangement at the first opportunity.

1

Some reflections on the background to Joyce's novels

HAVE you ever asked anyone what happens when they read a novel? Naturally, all sorts of responses are possible. Some might answer that in a novel they explore another world and escape into it. Some might say that they react with the characters in it, identifying closely with them, maybe responding to their actions, morally or emotionally perhaps. Others are absorbed by the plot, avidly following and anticipating its turns, while others again savour the background or the setting. And there are those too who rave about the language or the author's style.

In fact, I think as we read a novel we respond to all of these as well as to other aspects – and all at the same time. And it is always a personal response to the text. Different readers will come up with different views, interpretations, of the same text and even the same reader will react to the same text in a different way each time he or she reads it.

We each bring our own individual experiences to the text of a novel, and reading seems to me to be the process of interaction between the two. This is true whether we read for pleasure or because we must study a novel for an exam. However, studying a novel for an exam should not preclude the possibility of deriving pleasure from it. Indeed, I believe the opposite: that the point of studying a novel is really to increase the reader's pleasure from it. The aim should be to increase our awareness of how all these various aspects of a novel operate together, by examining features like themes, language, structure and background, and in such a way that our response is both broadened and intensified by our study.

I have stressed the importance of a *personal* response to the text of a novel, and I am convinced that before you go deeper into a novel by reading a study such as this one, you should make a record of your own feelings about it, especially your first impressions. This is vital because not only are your first impressions likely to be the most genuinely personal, but also because they are the most fleeting. In other words, once you start to read the views of critics your own impressions are likely to get quickly overlain by those of other people. This is even more important if you are studying for an exam because the examiner will be interested, above all, in your views: he/she wants to know what *you* think about the text in question. So before you start to read my views on Joyce make your own notes about what you find interesting or strange or even alarming about his books, and then we can move on. It is important to do that before you continue with this guide.

Reading Joyce's work

Joyce is one of the great names of 'culture'. Everyone has heard of him even if they have not read him. His reputation is such that he acts as a sort of ritual object in our culture, so much so that lots of people are actually put off reading his work. It is almost as if they feel belittled by his great stature. But reading Joyce is nowhere near as difficult as some people believe . . . and it is a great deal more fun too.

You will have discovered that he is not a conventional novelist, like Charles Dickens or Thomas Hardy, one who takes the reader firmly by the hand and fills out every detail in a novel, making almost everything in it explicit. Instead, Joyce expects the reader to work harder than most novelists do, not only to work out what is going on in a novel but also to decide on the significance of the goings-on. At the same time, he allows the reader a great deal more freedom in terms of interpreting and responding to a novel. As you may have already noticed, unlike most traditional writers he does not interfere by telling you how to react to the events and the people in his work. Freedom is one of the key features of his work in general and not all readers find this freedom easy to cope with at first.

Another unusual feature, related to this last point, which some-times disorientates new readers of Joyce, is his narrative style. Conventional readers often expect a novel to tell a story, with a strong plot-line, involving unexpected twists or complications which are nevertheless resolved by the author before the end, when a sense of stability is reimposed by him/her. Joyce's novels do not usually have this and even where there is a 'strong' narrative it tends to be a quite ordinary, low-key narrative, with a feeling that it arises naturally from the lives of ordinary people rather than being imposed on them. And typically there is never a convenient or final resolution of the plot; instead what we usually find at the end is a peculiar, eerie silence, which is usually a bit disconcerting, like the effect of a joke with no punchline. Which is probably very typical of life itself.

The very ordinariness of people's lives in Joyce's work can be a shock to the reader. Yet this ordinariness is only one facet of Joyce's unconventional approach in his writing. Have you noticed how much attention he gives in his novels to what goes on in the mind of a character – and how little to dramatic action or adventure? He is more concerned with what happens inside a character's mind and its reaction to events than with the events in themselves. And all of Joyce's works show this interest in the psychological realities of a person in preference to external considerations such as physical appearances. This is not to say that physical objects, settings and appearances are not important at all, but I would say that Joyce seldom describes things simply for their own sake. Almost always such external features appear as a way of exploring symbolically the consciousness of the character under attention, so that physical objects often take on an internal life of their own.

Thus Joyce's experiments with natural plot go hand-in-hand with his experiments in the exploration of inner mental realities. Joyce would say that the most important aspect of a novel or short story is not a dramatic plot or an exciting scene but people. People are always firmly in the foreground in Joyce, constantly before us. From beginning to end, in his life as in his art, Joyce is fascinated with the study of people, with their essence, their humanity, and above all with their consciousness. However, when Joyce began to write, at the beginning of the twentieth century, this was not the done thing. In order to explore this area of human activity he had to adopt unconventional, experimental modes of composition, and prominent among these are, as I am sure you have already found, his experiments in the use of language. I will be saying a good deal about these later, so for the time being I will say that although some readers find Joyce's language difficult, it is best to keep in mind the idea of freedom that I mentioned above and to read his texts openly at first, simply allowing the words to speak to you like music.

To enjoy Joyce's work all we need do is bring to it our own experience, our opinions and our interests. But to get a fully rounded vision it is necessary to consider the background to his writing. No writer writes in a vacuum, and a text inevitably grows out of a writer's own experience, opinions and interests, which are all formed by the circumstances of his/her own life and times. This is especially true of James Joyce and it is impossible to appreciate his achievement without becoming aware of the importance in Joyce's life of personal and public backgrounds, in particular the roles played by family, religion and politics.

Joyce the family man

All of Joyce's works have the 'family' at the centre. All of them demonstrate a vivid awareness of what it is to be a member of a family, with a deep sense of its roles and commitments, the tensions and emotions generated within family life and how that life is intensely concerned with the past and with the wider society around it. Joyce himself came from a close-knit family and inherited with it a strong sense of its past and, in particular, he was aware of how much it had declined during his own early life. His awareness of past prosperity appears to have induced in Joyce a deeper loyalty to the family both in his adolescence and in his own married life, and it forms the basis of a deeply rooted thematic concern in his work.

In general terms Joyce is very much an autobiographical novelist, in the sense that he repeatedly quarried his early family life for the material of his novels (though he often adapted this material to suit his artistic aims). His books seethe with the stresses generated by the profound ties of family loyalty, and at the same time he makes us very much aware of the critical dilemmas inherent in family life: the crisis of adolescence, the struggle for identity, the ties of fidelity, the threats to the family, the tensions between the individual and the family. And yet, what we are usually left with is also an image of the family as an oasis of love and regeneration, solace and hope.

Joyce's settings and perspectives (and even characters) are seldom stable and predictable, and his 'family' often seems to act as the microcosm of a world of flux. But always at the heart of this world of change and uncertainty is the solid, unwavering image of the mother, the great centre and resource of selfless love and assurance. Her presence is unmistakable, if understated, in all of his work.

Religious and political perspectives

The pervasive presence of the 'mother' in Joyce's writing derives principally, of course, from the dominant position of his own mother in his life. But it derives too from the prominent role played by the mother or madonna in the Roman Catholic Church, which had an enormously influential effect on Joyce's early life in Ireland. Although he later abandoned Catholicism for a more personal form of faith, the Church, like the family, thoroughly pervades the world of his writing. Joyce himself was profoundly aware of this, as we would expect, and his early work especially sets out to reveal the deep-rooted effects of the Church on the everyday lives and consciousness of his fellow Dubliners. But as you read his novels I think it is important for you to try to discover what Joyce's attitude is towards the Church: whether you think, for instance, that it is a force towards freedom and creativity, or instead towards inhibition and mediocrity, perhaps.

Joyce eventually abandoned the Catholic faith because he could no longer accept its fundamental doctrines. But he rejected it, too, out of artistic motives. He felt strongly that as an artist he could not fully and freely express his own true vision while he was in thrall to its monolithic authority. However, it was not enough simply to leave the Church, and eventually he quit Dublin as well as Ireland, to spend his adult life in what he regarded as a self-imposed 'exile' on the continent of Europe. And yet, in spite of this urge to escape, he returns again and again to the city in his writing: Dublin is the setting for practically every one of his texts.

On the other hand, his portraits of the city are never nostalgic or glamorised, in the way that expatriates often idealise their former homeland. His images of Dublin are starkly realistic. They are often ironic, and sometimes gloomy, and yet always sympathetic I believe, and this sympathy stems from Joyce's consciousness of the two great forces at work on the lives of ordinary Dubliners: the Church, of course, but also the British Empire.

Joyce did not take an active or explicit role in politics. A survey of his life and writing will reveal that his tendencies are generally socialist, humanistic and progressive. He was not particularly patriotic but he did look forward to the final liberation of Ireland, and he was undoubtedly proud of his Irish roots and of the achievements of past Irish artists. He considered British culture in general to be stultifying and moribund, lacking the vigour of its past and a victim of the complacent ease which had been engendered by centuries of cosy colonial power.

In Joyce's early years, his father had taken an active part in political life, and in Dublin at this time (about the end of the nineteenth century) there was a strong upsurge in the popular movement towards Home Rule for Ireland. Both of these aspects find their way into Joyce's novels. However, his father ultimately fell victim to the whims of political fortune, and the effect of this and of what he saw as the treachery of politicians was, I believe, to make Joyce extremely sceptical of politicians and of the political milieu. It represented for him a highly potential source of betrayal and, like established religion, a force more inclined to constrict and paralyse the mind of the artist than to liberate it.

The next step

The background to Joyce's work makes a fascinating study and if you would like to explore it in more detail I have listed several useful books on his contexts in the 'Further reading' section at the end of this book. An understanding of contexts will certainly increase your enjoyment of reading Joyce's novels, but I am sure that his work speaks well enough to a modern reader without the need for a lot of extraneous material. Joyce was writing for and about a modern world which is still with us, and his comic genius is as vibrant today as it was when his books were first published. Indeed, Joyce's increasing popularity is due chiefly to the fact that the human predicaments which he presents in his novels are both universal and timeless, while his famous literary experimentation continues to be a source of inspiration to modern writers.

The next step, then, is to address the novels themselves, to make a closely detailed study of the individual works. I have arranged them in the order of their composition partly to reveal the development of Joyce's very individual style, but also because it will make it easier to see how Joyce evolved his own vision or attitude towards the same themes and realities which recur throughout his life as an artist. For these same reasons I have also included Joyce's *Dubliners* in this study: while it is sometimes described simply as a collection of short stories, it is more than this and our study will reveal how in this early work Joyce adopted very much a novelistic approach. So, now we should begin to look in depth at the work of the man, and with the overall aim that by increasing our enjoyment of the individual works we can eventually appreciate why Joyce is considered by many to be the greatest writer of the twentieth century.

In order to achieve this we need to follow a method of analysis that will bring us close to the text and, at the same time, allow us to see the significance of Joyce's work. In the following chapters the method I will be using is that of taking a series of passages and gradually building a detailed view of the texts. I start by trying to get hold of the broad pattern of the book and then, step by step, I fill out my sense of that pattern by close analysis of passages from the text. All the time, the idea is to go from a simple sense of the text towards a more complex understanding of the way the text works.

At the heart of this method lie two points: that we need to see the large issues of the text, the large subjects Joyce is dealing with, but we also need to examine the particular way he brings these issues to life. In essence the method is to start with a general sense of the text, but then, through close analysis, to gain a particular sense of the way Joyce writes and how his language brings his themes to life. Of course, you may well disagree with the interpretations that I put forward and see very different things in the passages which are examined, but that is the point of this method: it allows you to focus on the text and, by examining it in detail, arrive at your own views and ideas about Joyce.

The method is, as you will see, used throughout the whole of this study, both for *Dubliners* and *A Portrait*, which are examined in considerable detail, and also for *Ulysses*, Joyce's epic novel which for many people remains the most important work of fiction of the twentieth century. Then, finally, I also look briefly at *Finnegans Wake*, a comic work of fascinating linguistic experiment, which is Joyce's most challenging text. However, as I hope to show, by tackling it in a methodical, logical way, we can not only come to terms with its difficulties but also enjoy its vitality and energy.

And this is the point of the disciplined study of texts: to gain more from them and from their individuality.

2

Dubliners: 'a nicely polished looking-glass'

I Constructing an overall analysis

ALTHOUGH *Dubliners* was the first of Joyce's prose works to be published, it was not at first conceived of as a coherent collection as such, with unifying themes and structure, nor even as a collection.

When Joyce's stories began to appear in a small Irish paper in August 1904 (starting with 'The Sisters'), they were the result of a commission from a friend to write some simple, interesting narratives of rural Irish life which might appeal to 'common understanding', and it was only during the following year that Joyce conceived of them in terms of a unified pattern with both a structured development and an overall purpose. He began to revise his sketches not only in terms of their individual meanings but also the relationships between stories.

Among the most important elements of all Joyce's writings is the role played by the city of Dublin itself and it is ironic that, although he finally left Ireland in 1904 for 'exile' in a multitude of cities around Europe, it is to Dublin that Joyce continually returns in his books. *Dubliners* marks the beginning of what is an ambivalent relationship with his city, a relationship in which he felt both contempt for the forces which subdued and deformed the souls of its people as well as a deep compassion for the victims of these forces. To fully express these conflicting responses, it was necessary for Joyce to create a convincing characterisation of the city, complete with its 'odour of ashpits and old weeds', as he himself put it, and to translate the ordinary substance of everyday Dublin lives into the radiant symbolic life of art. The following analysis sets out to explore the processes by which Joyce achieves these aims.

(1) After reading the book, think about the stories and what kind of pattern you can see in the text

When Joyce had determined his plan to fashion *Dubliners* as an integrated collection of stories, he explained his purpose to his brother: that the book would deal progressively with childhood, adolescence, adulthood and public life in Dublin. It is almost as if, in considering the city of Dublin, he was thinking in terms of the growth of a single human person with an identifiable character. Although Dublin at the turn of the century was, in Joyce's words, the 'second city' of the British Empire, its nature was still that of a large, overgrown village rather than an anonymous metropolis, so it readily lent itself to Joyce's project.

In the stories of childhood which open the book – 'The Sisters', 'An Encounter', 'Araby' – we are presented with a child's point of view, first of the family and then of other people, shown through the eyes of the unnamed boy who narrates them. It is a world of weariness and frustration, dominated by adults, but one which also holds out the promise of escape, first in the figure of Father Flynn and then in a day's 'miching' from school with two friends, in 'An Encounter'. In 'Araby', escape is suggested through both the exotic enchantment of the bazaar and the allure of Mangan's sister, who stirs the boy's latent sexuality. In all three stories Joyce locates the source of weariness and frustration in the cramped life of the adults who stifle the spirit of childhood and trap its impulse for flight.

The frustrations of these opening stories become more internalised in the next four, dealing with adolescence, although the origins of frustration are still distinct. In all four stories we witness young people struggling to make their own way against the benumbing influence of the older generation. 'Eveline' makes clear how strong the force exerted by the family can be in Dublin home life, and in 'After the Race' Jimmy Doyle is first an instrument of his father's half-formed social ambitions and then the victim of the sophisticated Europeans in his racing team, who exploit his naïvety. And we can see this theme of exploitation given extended treatment in the following two stories. In the ironically entitled 'Two Gallants', Corley's exploitation of his 'slavey' also serves to point up indirectly the weariness and sterility of the life of his companion, Lenehan, while 'The Boarding House' reverses the gender roles by making Bob Doran (and, to a lesser extent, Polly) the victim of the scheming Mrs Mooney who extracts full coin from the ensnared Bob Doran.

In the following four stories there is a deepening gloom with sketches of marital life, beginning with 'A Little Cloud' in which Little Chandler's awareness of the compromises in his life is intensified by a contrast with the rakish freedom of his old friend Ignatius Gallaher – a contrast which links this story with 'Two Gallants'. The decline of the spirit reaches its lowest point in this section of stories, first with the uncomfortable tale of Farrington ('Counterparts') and his simmering brutality which eventually erupts in an attack on his son, and then, two stories later, the 'Painful Case' of James Duffy and his rejection of Mrs Sinico's love. Between the two, 'Clay''s theme of the celibate life links it in part with 'A Painful Case', but its sketch of Maria's unfulfilled love gives it closer affinities with 'Eveline'.

The three stories of Dublin public life – 'Ivy Day in the Committee Room', 'A Mother', 'Grace' – concern, among other matters, the character of politics, culture and religion in Dublin, and it is not difficult to see that, in general terms, they are found lacking in genuine motivation and spirit. 'Grace' was to have been the final story in the collection but Joyce reflected with some shame that he had been too severe on his former hometown, and he wrote 'The Dead' to try to restore some balance, showing its more positive aspects, especially its hospitality and conscience, to set against the meaner side, with its pettiness, timidity and fatigue, which in any case Joyce regarded as the product of centuries of oppression by two empires, the Roman Catholic, principally, and the British.

Dubliners sets out to expose and explore the working of these forces on the souls of its citizens, revealing the grim realities of their lives. Nevertheless, while this necessarily throws up a good deal of ugliness, Joyce's expressed aim was ultimately positive, namely that he sought through these stories to give the Irish a good look at themselves in what he called his 'nicely polished looking-glass', as a first stage to bringing about a change in their lives. At the same time, his trenchant ironies weave a web of silent commentary throughout the collection, pointing up their crippling situations. These most often occur when one character's situation is paralleled by another, one setting off a 'comment' on the other; for example, consider the two mothers of 'A Boarding House' and 'A Mother', and the subtle ways in which their outcomes differ. Another source of Joyce's irony lies in the abruptness of his endings, which have the effect of leaving the reader in mid-air and of turning us back into the story to tie up the ends. A secondary effect of such endings is that our progress through the text is continually being arrested, not simply due to the episodic form of the collection, but also because we witness lives whose progress is invariably arrested by failure or hesitation.

A different form of irony issues from the gap between the stated ambitions of a character and his/her failure to achieve them, the gap between the ideals and realities of Dublin life. Such an irony usually depends on the blindness of the character to such gaps; in other words we observe the dreams of people such as Bob Doran or Chandler, fully aware, as they are not, that they have no chance of escaping their situations. It seems to me, too, that Joyce sets out to reveal the responsibility of some of the Dubliners themselves for their situation because either they avoid reflecting on themselves, or when they do reflect they fail to act – and, as Joyce said, the book itself is intended as a mirror for such reflections.

I have set out at length the emphasis which Joyce laid on the negative impulses of Dublin life and on its unglamorous facets. What, then, is the book's appeal? With so much denial, what gives *Dubliners* its interest? Well, to begin with, it is clear that much of the book's vitality derives from the moral tension arising from Joyce's exposure of these impulses. Furthermore, his exquisite ironies not only heighten this tension but also inject it with a wry-angled humour. *Dubliners* offers us Joyce's oblique comic vision, but the vision in turn depends for its ultimate effect on both a subtle delineation of character and on Joyce's own acute moral sensitivity, both of which help to give the work its strong appeal.

Equally important is Joyce's use of language, and in terms of verbal dexterity Joyce is unsurpassed. This dexterity is manifested in *Dubliners* in a variety of ways; these include an Irish musicality of expression and rhythm, an ear for the local idiom, and a knack of compelling the language to operate on both literal and symbolic levels simultaneously without any apparent strain of credibility. At the same time, for Joyce, language is multi-functional: a medium of presentation, a means of control as well as a fascination in itself.

Of his use of language in *Dubliners* Joyce wrote that he had adopted a 'style of scrupulous meanness', implying among other things a precise linguistic style. Equally, it can also suggest a spareness of detail – a critic writing at the time of publication said that in *Dubliners* Joyce 'carefully avoids telling you a lot you don't want to know'. He also avoids telling you a lot you might want to know, and an important feature of Joyce's attitude in *Dubliners*, which you have no doubt already encountered, is how much work he expects the reader to perform in filling out stories, finding and creating meanings. And yet the rewards for this invariably repay the effort put into his works.

Having said this, Joyce does offer what appear to be clues, parameters, to his own intentions. In *Dubliners* many of these cluster in the opening paragraph of 'The Sisters', where Joyce silently drops some hints to his approach in the collection as a whole. The boy of the story draws attention to them as strange words and they are set out in italics: *paralysis, gnomon, simony*. 'Paralysis' is, as we shall see, one of the most commonly occurring themes of the book. 'Simony' (the sin of making profit from the sale of religious offices, pardons and so on) is expressed often metaphorically in a broad variety of ways, from Father Purdon's materialistic sermon in 'Grace' to the political compromises of 'Ivy Day in the Committee Room'. The word 'gnomon' refers literally to the pointer on a sundial but also, more importantly to that part of a geometric figure remaining after a section has been removed from it. Applied to *Dubliners* then, 'gnomon' suggests Joyce's technique of omitting pieces from his stories, his gaps and silences; for example, the boy of the opening stories is unnamed, a key verse is missing from Maria's song at the end of 'Clay' and important people are absent from the story 'Ivy Day in the Committee Room'. In general, of course, 'gnomon' refers to those crucial elements which the reader him/herself brings to and contributes to the stories.

This dip into the opening paragraph of 'The Sisters' serves as a good introduction to the work as a whole and, armed with these general pointers, we can now take a closer look at the stories themselves.

(2) Select a short passage from the opening story, 'The Sisters', and try to build upon the ideas you have established so far

I have decided to take a close look at a passage from the opening pages of this story, in which the young boy who narrates it describes a conversation between the adults around him, revealing that his friend, the old priest Father Flynn, has just died.

> Old Cotter was sitting at the fire, smoking, when I came downstairs to supper. While my aunt was ladling out my stirabout he said, as if returning to some former remark of his:
>   – No, I wouldn't say he was exactly . . . but there was something queer . . . there was something uncanny about him. I'll tell you my opinion. . . .
>   He began to puff at his pipe, no doubt arranging his opinion in his mind. Tiresome old fool! When we knew him first he used to be rather interesting, talking of faints and worms; but I soon grew tired of him and his endless stories about the distillery.
>   – I have my own theory about it, he said. I think it was one of those . . . peculiar cases. . . . But it's hard to say. . . .
>   He began to puff again at his pipe without giving us his theory. My uncle saw me staring and said to me:
>   – Well, so your old friend is gone, you'll be sorry to hear.
>   – Who? said I.
>   – Father Flynn.
>   – Is he dead?
>   – Mr Cotter here has just told us. He was passing by the house.
>   I knew that I was under observation so I continued eating as if the news had not interested me. My uncle explained to old Cotter.
>   – The youngster and he were great friends. The old chap taught him a great deal, mind you; and they say he had a great wish for him.
>   – God have mercy on his soul, my aunt said piously.
>   Old Cotter looked at me for a while. I felt that his little beady black eyes were examining me but I would not satisfy him by looking up from my plate. He returned to his pipe and finally spat rudely into the grate.
>   – I wouldn't like children of mine, he said, to have too much to say to a man like that.
>   – How do you mean, Mr Cotter? asked my aunt.
>   – What I mean is, said old Cotter, it's bad for children. My idea is: let a young lad run about and play with young lads of his own age and not be . . . Am I right, Jack?
>   That's my principle, too, said my uncle. Let him learn to box his corner. That's what I'm always saying to that Rosicrucian there: take exercise. Why, when I was a nipper every morning of my life I had a cold bath, winter and summer. And that's what stands to me now. Education is all very fine and large. . . . Mr Cotter might take a pick of that leg of mutton, he added to my aunt.
>
> [*Dubliners* (Penguin, 1992) pp. 1–2]

When you try to analyse a passage such as this it is a good idea to have a plan. This will help you to structure your reading and enable you to read with a purpose. I will say more in detail in the next chapter about formulating a plan, but for the moment I would like to suggest that we start by looking for an opposition or conflict in the passage. This is important because all narrative literature depends for its interest to some extent on the tension which arises from the conflicts within it and this can usually be seen on every page of a novel or short story. Such tension helps to reveal vital information about the characters involved and it is also important in setting out the themes and interest of the work; in fact, tensions within a book can often determine the form of the whole work. Therefore, if your plan sets out to uncover the oppositions or conflicts in a work, it can offer an effective method of penetrating and understanding the complexities of a passage, and ultimately, by analysing a series of such passages, you can form a comprehensive picture of the whole text. For this reason, we will be building up our study of Joyce's texts by looking closely at some selected passages from them.

In the first passage, above, old Cotter is giving his opinion about Father Flynn, to whom the boy in the story was especially close. What we learn about old Cotter is that he is a crafty, opinionated windbag who is free with his gossiping, at least according to the image presented by the narrator. There is a kind of cat-and-mouse game going on between the boy and old Cotter, the boy pretending not to pay attention to the old man's testing words while old Cotter scrutinises the boy's reactions with his 'beady black eyes'. The boy refuses to acknowledge his own feelings for the priest in front of the adults and denies old Cotter the satisfaction of knowing he is the first to break the news about the priest's death.

The boy makes clear the conflict between himself and old Cotter with his description of him as a 'Tiresome old fool!', but we can detect it anyway in the way that the boy refuses to rise to old Cotter's bait and to the gossip about the priest. The air in the room seems tense for the boy, caught between his loyalty to Father Flynn and his contempt for Mr Cotter. The adults appear as a paralysing constraint on his spirit with their stifling opinions of the priest and their moralising advice on bringing up children. It is clear, too, that although Mr Cotter and Uncle Jack are talking to each other, they are really addressing their remarks to the silent, indignant boy whom they patronise in this way as a child.

This passage comes near the start of the story and although we learn some important points, such as the names of some of the characters and something of their relationships, a great air of mystery still hangs about the opening few pages – and it still hangs about at the end. One of the main causes of the mystery is old Cotter, who has a habit of not finishing his sentences: 'I'll tell you my opinion . . . ' and 'But it's hard to say . . . '. By saying that he would not like children to have too much to say to a 'man like that', he not only patronises the boy but also, of course, raises suspicions about Father Flynn. It is curious that even though the story's title points us in the direction of the sisters as the focus of the story, it is Father Flynn who is at its centre, and he never appears directly in it. His absence has the effect of increasing the mystery surrounding him and from the words of these two men at the start we might begin to suspect that there was something immoral about the priest. All of these points are skilfully manipulated by Joyce at the start of the story to draw us into its intriguing scenario.

Ironically, in one way we are placed in something like the same position in the story as the boy himself – in terms of a lack of information about what the priest did which old Cotter took exception to. A clue to this is given by the boy's uncle Jack when he says 'Education is all very fine and large . . . ' (though he too does not finish this sentence). His uncle has explained that the boy and the priest were great friends and the boy had been taught a great deal. We discover later what sort of things Father Flynn had taught him, and that among many other things he had revealed something of the mysteries of the Church and the significance of its institutions (including the 'secrecy of the confession') which seem so profound that the boy is stunned. With this in mind we can see more clearly the difference between what old Cotter and the priest individually represent to the boy. On the one hand, old Cotter and Uncle Jack with their overprotective moralising and their proposals of exercise and cold baths represent an addled and paralysing world of ignorance and inhibition which offers little or no concessions to the expanding mind of the boy. On the other hand, the revelations of the priest represent a universe of challenge and release, encouraging the boy to know more. In a word, Father Flynn does not treat him as a child to be kept in protective ignorance as the other adults do, but initiates him into something of the mysterious world of grown-ups, offering secret and possibly forbidden knowledge. The boy is liberated through the priest's illumination while the evasive utterances of old Cotter and Uncle Jack foreshadow a realm of ignorance and constraint.

As I noted above, in our uncertainty of what is happening we are in a position similar to that of the boy in the story, of being kept in the dark, but perhaps even more so since what we learn is limited to what he himself discovers and then decides to reveal to us. And this is another source of tension in this story – the fact that we feel we are continually being kept at arm's length from the centre of the story: namely, the apparent scandal of the priest (even the boy describes him as a 'simoniac'). The oblique title is just one instance of the way that we are deflected away from this central point, and the unfinished sentences, half-heard rumours, silences and shadowy settings all contribute. Joyce's style, too, seems evasive, by not filling in details, though his language is skilfully attuned to the musicality of Irish dialogue and the local idiom. He also has a way of getting the language to work on both literal and symbolic levels without any strain of credibility, and this enhances the mystery here and later in the story (for instance, the 'faints and worms' in the passage refer to the equipment of a distillery but metaphorically they also imply that old Cotter is devious). So when, later, we do reach a point of revelation, when Eliza tells us that the priest had gone mad after breaking a chalice and that the chalice was empty (it 'held nothing'), we can rightly see in the chalice a symbol of the Catholic Church itself, and that Father Flynn, trapped and paralysed by his commitment to an empty faith, had become unhinged. Perhaps it is for this reason that old Cotter wants to protect the boy from 'a man like that'.

(3) Select a second passage for discussion

The second passage I have chosen is taken from the opening page of 'Eveline'.

> She sat at the window watching the evening invade the avenue. Her head was leaned against the window curtains and in her nostrils was the odour of dusty cretonne. She was tired.
>
> Few people passed. The man out of the last house passed on his way home; she heard his footsteps clacking along the concrete pavement and afterwards crunching on the cinder path before the new red houses. One time there used to be a field there in which they used to play every evening with other people's children. Then a man from Belfast bought the field and built houses in it – not like their little brown houses but bright brick houses with shining roofs. The children of the avenue used to play together in that field – the Devines, the Waters, the Dunns, little Keogh the cripple, she and her brothers and sisters. Ernest, however, never played: he was too grown up. Her father used often to hunt them in out of the field with his blackthorn stick; but usually little Keogh used to keep *nix* and call

out when he saw her father coming. Still they seemed to have been rather happy then. Her father was not so bad then; and besides, her mother was alive. That was a long time ago; she and her brothers and sisters were all grown up; her mother was dead. Tizzie Dunn was dead, too, and the Waters had gone back to England. Everything changes. Now she was going to go away like the others, to leave her home.

Home! She looked round the room, reviewing all its familiar objects which she had dusted once a week for so many years, wondering where on earth all the dust came from. Perhaps she would never see again those familiar objects from which she had never dreamed of being divided. And yet during all those years she had never found out the name of the priest whose yellowing photograph hung on the wall above the broken harmonium beside the colour print of the promises made to Blessed Margaret Mary Alacoque. He had been a school friend of her father. Whenever he showed the photograph to a visitor her father used to pass it with a casual word:

– He is in Melbourne now.

[pp. 29–30]

'Eveline' is one of Joyce's stories of adolescence. It is narrated exclusively from the eponymous heroine's point of view, almost completely from the window through which she gazes on the world going past. Outside, very little seems to happen: 'Few people passed.' But it represents an 'otherness' and a desire which seduces Eveline from her home with its 'odour of dusty cretonne'. Her home is characterised by this dustiness which she cleans and has cleaned every week for years. The dust is set up as a sort of prison for her in its inescapability, the monotony of its inevitability and also in its hints of the decay about the house – her mother and brother Ernest are dead, while others have escaped, and there are the colours brown and yellow, which in Joyce's work usually signify decay and paralysis. 'Everything changes', she reflects, but not for Eveline, not now at least.

Yet the opening paragraphs also set up the possibility of escape from this isolation as her thoughts move out into the street and the past and then return to home and the dust, and then out again. Further, the movement helps set up the mood of hesitation, a feature both of Eveline's state of mind and of Joyce's technique in this story, setting up its central tensions. As she looks outside of her cell-like window, her thoughts escape to the past, the new red houses contrasting with their own old brown ones. It was a golden period when she 'seemed to have been rather happy' – but notice the tone of reservation or hesitation even in this happy recollection. Home was a haven then and she mixed with other people.

But change is also a key word in the second paragraph, though for Eveline it is equated with decline, and the metaphorical force of the final four sentences is unmistakable. Eveline has been left behind.

In the third paragraph, her attention switches to the room as the exclamation 'Home!' beckons her back to the familiar objects of her life. There is also the first indication of what she might be leaving behind. Yet the terms in which Joyce presents this possibility also imply her dread of leaving, especially in the repetition of 'never', which like the words 'dust' and 'home' work to define the strict limits of what she can aspire to. As the second paragraph indicates, it is other people who do things, who go away. The yellowing photograph of the priest who left for Melbourne reminds us of the constant religious background, as do the promises made to Blessed Margaret Mary Alacoque, a saint who eschewed marriage for a life of service and persecution.

Eveline's home is a prison typified not only by decay and servitude. We also learn of her father's brutality, chiefly towards her brother in the past, but increasingly she feels the threat is towards herself. And even in the happy past her father used to hunt them in with a stick. Now she is exploited by him: she hands over her entire wages to him and is insulted into the bargain. Further, she compounds this by taking on the role of holding together the family, a role taken on from her dead mother who appears to have become insane by the end, uttering incomprehensible or nonsensical Irish on her deathbed [p. 33]. The implication is, of course, that the demands of the father and the family had driven her to it – it is a familiar tension in Joyce: between the selfish dissolute men breaking up the family and the women who work to hold it together (compare Maria in 'Clay' and Mrs Kernan in 'Grace', and in 'The Sisters' the women are left to pick up and pull the pieces together after the break-up and death of Father Flynn). Eveline promised to her dying mother to 'keep the home together' [p. 33] and her promise is one more compromise binding her to the home.

Set against the sombre prospect of this background, Frank offers a haven, escape and adventure, a baulk against the stifling repression of home: 'He would save her' [p. 42]. He is associated with the alternative life which beckons: together they see the operetta *The Bohemian Girl* (one of the many ironic touches in the story) and they sit in an unfamiliar part of the theatre. He wins her through stories of strange places and, as if to convince her of the rightness of Frank, her possessive father forbids her to see him; yet it only works to intensify their affair since they are now forced to meet secretly. Eveline's choice of words to refer to Frank reveal his appeal for her: unaccustomed, excitement, distant, different, secretly; and when he sings she becomes pleasantly 'confused' (a word which in *Dubliners* is usually associated with mild sexual arousal). His home in 'Buenos Ayres', where he had apparently fallen on his feet, sets up an ironic contrast with its hope of 'good airs' against the odour of dust in her home.

But all may not be as it seems. After all, we have only Frank's word for his having 'fallen on his feet'. And this is an important aspect of Joyce's narrative point of view in this story. Everything is narrated to us through the naïve eyes of nineteen-year-old Eveline who is enchanted by exotic sailor stories. And her father warns the reader, as well as Eveline, 'I know these sailor chaps.'

Frank may be anything but frank. We know more about Eveline and we know that she is the sort of gullible, inexperienced maiden who could be duped by smooth sailor talk, and she is susceptible to his charms (the childlike idiom of her thoughts in the above extract suggests she may also be slightly retarded). If they were to sail away together, then their first stop would be Liverpool, which was notorious as a place to which many Irish Evelines had been drawn by sailors like Frank and then abandoned to a life of poverty and, often, prostitution. So for Eveline, the dilemma may be a choice between two lives of male exploitation, although she does not realise it.

Another irony of Eveline's predicament is that in spite of her father's treatment of her, she still feels obligated to him. She is aware of his need for her, she has been made to feel indispensable to him, in part through her promises and in part through her ready adoption of the role of the server: she notices how old he looks and that 'He would miss her' [p. 32]. Her optimistic nature repeatedly balances the cheerlessness of her situation against her perception of its homely security, bringing about another opposition in the story. So after her thoughts have dwelt on the unpleasantness of her home, she reminds herself of its familiar cosiness ('She knew the air') and then, following thoughts of her father's truculence and the consuming 'demands' of home, she recalls his kindnesses to her [p. 32].

Fundamentally, Eveline's own psychology is an integral part of her predicament. She has a profound uncertainty about her identity and she appears to have little other than that which is imposed by other people. We have seen how her family have imposed on her the role of server, seeing herself through their eyes, and her life at the Stores appears to be the same [p. 30]. In a strangely disembodied way she wonders what they would say after they discovered she had eloped, and concludes that they would call her a fool. The hollowness of her identity is confirmed by her reflection that 'her place would be filled up by advertisement' [p. 30]. She even surprises herself with the prospect of imposing herself on the world, albeit by marriage: 'people would treat her with respect then', she reflects [p. 30] – marriage would be a sort of revenge on them. The truth is that she needs someone else, now Frank, who could redefine her persona. Her own passivity contrasts with her romanticised version of Frank as a self-made adventurer, and Eveline lives through him and his prospects. The resounding emptiness in her soul becomes increasingly apparent.

And then we see her by the North Wall, confronted by the beckoning figure of Frank himself. Or do we? Does she actually go to the North Wall, the point of departure for Liverpool, Buenos Ayres . . . who knows where? Or does the final page take place only in Eveline's imagination, where so much of the story takes place?

The climax of the story brilliantly draws Eveline's crisis to its head. She now finds herself cowed by the two irreconcilable forces of her home and her lover, the two contradictory impulses which nullify each other as well as Eveline herself. She is trapped 'like a helpless animal' [p. 34] and, consistent with what we have seen, depicts her dilemma not as a choice between different futures for herself but between two duties to other people. She prays to God for guidance – she cannot even consult her own conscience. Confused, she is again paralysed, bereft by these forces of any life-will which would impose a direction from within. And the scene eventually climaxes as she seems to undergo something like an orgasm in the silent ecstasy of prayer before she sends out her 'cry of anguish' [p. 34].

Joyce's masterstroke lies in the uncertainty of the closure: is she really at the dockside, does she leave with Frank after all? These come on top of all the other uncertainties which the narrator, using Eveline's point of view, has fostered. Joyce's own silence, by ending the story at this point, skilfully places the reader within the heroine's dilemma and makes the focus of the story Eveline's crippled, ineffectual consciousness, the product of the oppressing forces around her: religion, and the male-centred home.

(4) Select a third passage for discussion

The third passage I have chosen for discussion is taken from 'A Painful Case', one of Joyce's stories of adulthood.

> Mr Duffy abhorred anything which betokened physical or mental disorder. A mediaeval doctor would have called him saturnine. His face, which carried the entire tale of his years, was of the brown tint of Dublin streets. On his long and rather large head grew dry black hair and a tawny moustache did not quite cover an unamiable mouth. His cheek bones also gave his face a harsh character; but there was no harshness in the eyes which, looking at the world from under their tawny eyebrows, gave the impression of a man ever alert to greet a redeeming instinct in others but often disappointed. He lived at a little distance from his body, regarding his own acts with doubtful side-glances. He had an odd autobiographical habit which led him to compose in his mind from time to time a short sentence about himself containing a subject in the third person and a predicate in the past tense. He never gave alms to beggars and walked firmly, carrying a stout hazel.
>
> He had been for many years cashier of a private bank in Baggot Street. Every morning he came in from Chapelizod by tram. At midday he went to Dan Burke's and took his lunch – a bottle of lager beer and a small trayful of arrowroot biscuits. At four o'clock he was set free. He dined in an eating-house in George's Street where he felt himself safe from the society of Dublin's gilded youth and where there was a certain plain honesty in the bill of fare. His evenings were spent either before his landlady's piano or roaming about the outskirts of the city. His liking for Mozart's music brought him sometimes to an opera or a concert: these were the only dissipations of his life.
>
> He had neither companions nor friends, church nor creed. He lived his spiritual life without any communion with others, visiting his relatives at Christmas and escorting them to the cemetery when they died. He performed these two social duties for old dignity's sake but conceded nothing further to the conventions which regulate the civic life. He allowed himself to think that in certain circumstances he would rob his bank but, as these circumstances never arose, his life rolled out evenly – an adventureless tale.
>
> One evening he found himself sitting beside two ladies in the Rotunda. The house, thinly peopled and silent, gave distressing prophecy of failure. The lady who sat next him looked round at the deserted house once or twice and then said:
>
> – What a pity there is such a poor house tonight! It's so hard on people to have to sing to empty benches.

[pp. 104–5]

I have chosen this passage from the story because, following a description of the situation and the lodging room of its main character, Mr Duffy, Joyce now focuses more closely on the man himself.

One of the most striking features of this passage is the repetition of negative elements, a feature that recurs throughout *Dubliners* (compare the opening to 'The Sisters': 'There was no hope for him this time . . . '). The repetition creates an insistent down-beat that stifles any hope. His mouth is 'unamiable' and 'harsh', he is frequently 'disappointed' and he 'never gave alms to beggars'. Such repetition is a key feature of *Dubliners* as a whole, where it is used to reinforce the themes of monotony, entrapment and paralysis. Here the repetition of negative aspects also works to underline both his monotonous life and his dogmatism – his is an 'adventureless tale', but it is adventureless because of his wilful denial. He appears to have tried to eradicate all the normal impulses and vitality from life.

His life is governed by routine: every day he travels in from the outskirts by tram, eats his meals in the same places where he eats the same things (four years later, after the death of Mrs Sinico, he is still taking his lunch in George's Street). The impression we receive is that, like Maria in the preceding story, 'Clay', Duffy is well established in the routine of his life and consoled by the firm control he exerts over it. Unlike Maria, however, who is disappointed by her own celibacy, Mr Duffy is content with his solitary and highly disciplined life (he 'abhorred anything which betokened physical or mental disorder' [p. 104]). It is this austere physical and emotional order which Mrs Sinico will invade and disrupt with the offer of love that she brings. However, for the time being, his life is strictly regulated.

In the opening pages of the story, we have a description of Mr Duffy's cell, a refuge on the outskirts of Dublin, cut off from human contact, whose interior is cold and utilitarian, lacking both vividness and ornament. And then in the first paragraph of our extract Joyce focuses attention on how Mr Duffy's own appearance mirrors this lack of colour (there are the colours which Joyce associates with sickness or stagnation – yellow, tawny, buff and brown, and the name 'Duffy' may be taken from the Irish adjective *dubh*, meaning 'black'). Just as he lives on the edge of Dublin, he lives 'at a little distance from his body', about which he is suspicious. He is not only an extremely regulated man but he fears the sexuality of his own body, threatening to overturn his strict discipline and disrupt his puritanical order. It is this mortifying fear of sexuality and anything resembling passion which eventually prompts him to reject Mrs Sinico (after she had impetuously pressed his hand to her cheek [p. 107]), as a threat to his regime, though we feel it would have a humanising effect on him as a whole; instead, he ponderously declares that ' . . . friendship between man and woman is impossible because there must be sexual intercourse' [p. 108]. This, of course, throws up the opposition in their expectations of the relationships: Mrs Sinico seeks and offers love, Mr Duffy seeks merely fellowship.

The second paragraph sets out the details of the monotony of Mr Duffy's routine at work and his taste for 'plain' honest fare, again a reflection of himself as a plain man. His only regular social involvement is the opera, but notice how Joyce's use of the word 'dissipation' associates amusement with moral degradation, as if Mr Duffy regards other such activities as morally degrading. In this paragraph two interesting points serve to indicate that, while Mr Duffy's life is rigorously ordered, we get no sense that there is any genuine direction for his existence. His disciplinary controls are not marshalled around any moral principle, the discipline is not directed towards any particular goal or motivated by any inward spirituality (he has neither 'church nor creed'). It seems to be for its own sake, an expression of his puritanical turn of mind.

He is 'set free' from work at four o'clock, implying that his work at the bank is a trap, a drudgery; yet, after he is set free he often spends his time 'roaming the outskirts of the city', ironically suggesting a drifting, timorous life, afraid to engage with the heart of the city. For a time at least, Mrs Sinico and the possibility of fellowship give it some focal point.

In the third paragraph we see Mr Duffy in relation to others and we discover there, as we might have expected, the same negativity and denial. He has no friends and he actively avoids contact or 'communion'. His social calendar is limited to visits to relatives at Christmas. Even his attendance at the funerals of his relatives is exercised out of a perfunctory sense of duty, and this cold acknowledgement of anything resembling a social convention is singular. With heavy irony, Joyce reveals that he has contemplated robbing his bank, but it is impossible for us to envisage how such a timorous, withdrawn and saturnine individual could be fired up to do this, or to comprehend how extreme the 'circumstances' would have to be to bring this about. Or, indeed, what Mr Duffy might do with the money.

So it is the lacklustre 'life' of this empty shell of a man that Mrs Sinico will penetrate, and Joyce's objective style has more than prepared the way. At the concert he 'found himself sitting . . . ', a description which implies that he does not really have any active aim or expectations of the occasion. The prophecy of failure and the thinly peopled house seem in effect to be extensions of Mr Duffy's ethos itself. And then Mrs Sinico speaks to him and we notice immediately the contrast with what has gone before. This is in direct speech (the only such example, if we discount that in the newspaper on page 110, which is in any case reported) and signals life and engagement, communion with others. Notice also the emotion expressed in her words 'What a pity . . . ' and 'It's so hard on people . . . '; these reveal the two gifts that Mrs Sinico offers to Duffy: communion and feeling – which he rejects with lethal consequences.

We have noted above how Joyce's own objective style here acts as a parallel to Mr Duffy's cold, imperturbable nature. This, we have said, withholds sympathy for the man, yet Joyce does not intrude anywhere in the story to make a direct moral comment on or against him. Instead, Joyce relies for his effect on irony; for instance, both Mr Duffy's rigorous discipline and his impassiveness are so unremitting that he becomes ultimately a parody of himself. The irony is increased by Mr Duffy's failure to reflect on himself except in a blinkered sort of way, especially with regard to his self-contradictions. For example, we are told he seemed 'ever alert to greet a redeeming instinct in others', but this is hideously belied by his treatment of Mrs Sinico. His apparent interest in socialism seems equally unlikely, and we wonder what he hoped to find at the meetings of the Irish Socialist Party.

In making clearer the narrator's dislike of him, the irony also intensifies the isolation of Mr Duffy. At the start of the story, it is his solitude which is pronounced, but by the conclusion, after the realisation of his part in Mrs Sinico's death, the emphasis is on his loneliness. The movement between these two points also traces the progression to its logical conclusion of Mr Duffy's withdrawal from life. The word 'lone' together with its derivatives recur throughout the story until we reach the final word, and its chilling sound reverberates in the silence beyond the close of the story: 'He felt that he was alone' [p. 114].

The end of the story is a brilliant moment of heightened consciousness: the consciousness of the living becoming infused by the presence of the dead. The final paragraphs of the story are superbly worked, as Mr Duffy's increasing awareness of the sterility of his spirit interweaves with the memory of the dead woman and the life of her spirit. It is his growing awareness of this intricate relationship and the immanence of the dead which invokes his gradual realisation of the horror of what has happened: 'She seemed to be near him in the darkness' [p. 113].

These moments in which a character and the reader see into the truth of what is happening, a sudden luminescent reality, are a characteristic feature of Joyce's work and are used in *Dubliners*, in varying degrees of intensity, as a method of communicating inner states. Furthermore, because they involve moments of heightened consciousness, they have a structural role in creating the climax of a story. Joyce later gave the term 'epiphany', a 'showing forth', to such moments, and in addition to their function of exposing reality they also often have a moral role in the sense that through them a character comes to reflect and comment on himself.

Here, the final two pages trace this gradual realisation by Duffy, his private 'epiphany', in which he sees the truth of what has happened – that Mrs Sinico's ignominious death, far from being an indictment of her life, is in effect an indictment of his own. Ironically, the epiphany works through the very faculty – his ego – which had earlier vilified her, because it causes him to reflect on his self, his loneliness, as an 'outcast from life's feast' [p. 113]. The silence of the night and the receding memory of Mrs Sinico (which underlines the receding hope of any redemption) coincide with the awareness of his having cast himself from life's rich feast. And, with the final words 'He felt that he was alone', we are left with the impression that the simoniac at last confronts the terror of the emptiness of his soul.

(5) Select a fourth passage for discussion

The fourth passage I have selected is from 'Grace', one of the stories of Dublin public life, and occurs at a point in the story after Mr Kernan has collapsed in the toilets of a Dublin bar. He has retired to his bed to recuperate.

Two nights after his friends came to see him. She brought them up to his bedroom, the air of which was impregnated with a personal odour, and gave them chairs at the fire. Mr Kernan's tongue, the occasional stinging pain of which had made him somewhat irritable during the day, became more polite. He sat propped up in the bed by pillows and the little colour in his puffy cheeks made them resemble warm cinders. He apologized to his guests for the disorder of the room but at the same time looked at them a little proudly.

He was quite unconscious that he was the victim of a plot which his friends, Mr Cunningham, Mr M'Coy and Mr Power had disclosed to Mrs Kernan in the parlour. The idea had been Mr Power's but its development was entrusted to Mr Cunningham. Mr Kernan came of Protestant stock and, though he had been converted to the Catholic faith at the time of his marriage, he had not been in the pale of the Church for twenty years. He was fond, moreover, of giving side-thrusts at Catholicism.

Mr Cunningham was the very man for such a case. He was an elder colleague of Mr Power. His own domestic life was not very happy. People had great sympathy with him for it was known that he had married an unpresentable woman who was an incurable drunkard. He had set up house for her six times; and each time she had pawned the furniture on him.

Everyone had respect for poor Martin Cunningham. He was a thoroughly sensible man, influential and intelligent. His blade of human knowledge, natural astuteness particularised by long association with cases in the police courts, had been tempered by brief immersions in the waters of general philosophy. He was well informed. His friends bowed to his opinions and considered that his face was like Shakespeare's.

When the plot had been disclosed to her Mrs Kernan had said:
– I leave it all in your hands, Mr Cunningham.

After a quarter of a century of married life she had very few illusions left. Religion for her was a habit and she suspected that a man of her husband's age would not change greatly before death. She was tempted to see a curious appropriateness in his accident and, but that she did not wish to seem bloody-minded, she would have told the gentlemen that Mr Kernan's tongue would not suffer by being shortened. However, Mr Cunningham was a capable man; and religion was religion. The scheme might do good and, at least, it could do no harm. Her beliefs were not extravagant. She believed steadily in the Sacred Heart as the most generally useful of all Catholic devotions and approved of the sacraments. Her faith was bounded by her kitchen but, if she were put to it, she could believe in the banshee and in the Holy Ghost.

The gentlemen began to talk of the accident . . .

[pp. 156–7]

I have chosen this passage from 'Grace', a story of public life, because it comes at a key moment in the story when a conspiracy to entice Tom Kernan back to the 'pale' of the Catholic Church is mooted by the narrator. This moment in the story forms a transitional stage during which descriptions of people are sorted out, and theme and plot begin to take a more distinct form. After the degraded image of drunken Mr Kernan having fallen downstairs into the basement lavatory of a bar (where he lay smeared in filth and ooze, making 'a grunting noise' [p. 149]), his physical recovery is set up, and then the narrative begins to turn its attention to the future, giving momentum to the later parts of the story. The change is underlined subtly by the narrator's choice of words, in the repeated use of the adverb/preposition 'up' in the first paragraph – Mrs Kernan takes his friends 'up to his bedroom', and the man himself is 'propped up' in bed (an opposing thread is set up through the story by the repetition of the words 'fall' and 'fail'). On the other hand, the disorder of the room reminds us of the recent disorder of his life, and by apologising for this he discloses the change in his attitude; however, the plot insists that he is yet to order his own life and that of his family. The fire and the warm colour of his cheeks signify health and conviviality, of course, but with a feint ironic hint of the hell from which he has been saved.

This passage occurs as one stage, that of Kernan's fall from grace, is finished, and the next stage, his recovery to grace, is about to begin. But the word 'grace' has varied meanings in the story. Besides the conventional religious sense of a spiritual state of purity, it also carries the sense of dignity or 'social decorum'. Both meanings are clearly relevant here, and so is the meaning of the word in the business expression, 'a period of grace', an extended period of time allowed to an individual to settle a debt. So Mr Kernan has been saved, for the time being, and this transitional period marks the period of grace for him to set his house in order. A recovery, of sorts, is about to begin.

Although Mr Power promises Mrs Kernan to 'make a new man of him . . . ' [p. 154], they actually set out to make an old man of him in the sense of his former self and this is important; it is to be a *retreat*, as they say. It is equally important to remember that Joyce does not play on the spiritual condition of Kernan so much as on his outward appearance or image. The central idea here is that of 'decorum' and this, too, is expressed in a variety of ways. 'Grace' as decorum refers to Mr Kernan's social standing and in particular the need for these businessmen to appear respectable, creating an outward semblance of grace. Such an idea is consistent with Mr Kernan's strongly élitist attitude shown in his snobbery against the rural vulgarity of Dublin's country policemen and priests. The Jesuits, too, appear élitist both here and elsewhere in Joyce. The prose in the story also has a decorum, an aloofness as well as a conventional regularity and precision in both the vocabulary and sentence construction (for instance, consider the paragraph above which begins 'After a quarter of a century . . . '). But, above all, in this story decorum is associated with conformity, both religious and social, and this forms the basis of Joyce's subtle comic effect.

A key indication of Joyce's interest in the story comes with the appearance of the word 'respect', in the middle of our extract, referring to Martin Cunningham's public standing. This description of his own impeccable social status, coming so soon after Kernan's degradation, is part of the moral function of the story. Notice the acclaim accorded Cunningham: thoroughly sensible, influential, intelligent, naturally astute, well-informed; and his friends defer to his opinion. This is later undermined by the narrator, particularly in that Cunningham is misinformed, and misinforming, in the dispute about the Church (he gets the 'mottoes' of the popes wrong and he mistakes the identities of the churchmen who voted against the doctrine of 'infallibility' [pp. 166–7 and 169]). But what is stressed, for the time being anyway, is Mr Cunningham's moral image among other Dubliners, his grace, as a contrast to Kernan's lack of it.

'Grace' in the sense of 'decorum' is epitomised by Mr Kernan's silk hat, the essential appurtenance of his trade and the badge of his standing within his bourgeois society. Joyce subtly charts the odyssey of this hat from the beginning; for example, on the opening page it has rolled away on the filthy floor of the lavatory, 'dinged' (which carries the implication of 'dingy' as well as 'dented') then retrieved and carried upstairs by a bystander [p. 149]. Eventually, this 'battered silk hat' is replaced on Mr Kernan's head just before he is rescued by Mr Power [p. 150]. Its significance as a badge of his grace and status is made clear shortly after his rescue by Mr Power:

> Mr Kernan was a commercial traveller of the old school which believed in the *dignity* of its calling. He had never been seen in the city without a silk hat of some decency and a pair of gaiters. By *grace* of these two articles of clothing, he said, a man could always pass muster.
>
> [pp. 152–3; my emphasis]

Reinforcing this idea, Mrs Kernan recalls how decorously he had appeared at their wedding, wearing his silk hat 'gracefully' [p. 155]. At the end, Mr Kernan's return to respectability is signalled by the appearance of his 'rehabilitated' hat, resting on his

knees in church [p. 172], as 'Mr Kernan restored his hat to its original position' [p. 173].

As I said before, Mr Cunningham is admired and respected, by
his associates, chiefly for his intelligence but also for his exem-
plary moral behaviour in continuing to maintain his drunkard
wife – a predicament which is also the source of some sympathy
for 'poor Martin Cunningham'. But, if we look more closely, we
can see that there is some irony here, although it is by no means
certain whose opinion we are given in the passage. The language
in the paragraph beginning 'Mr Cunningham was the very
man . . . ' has the air of another character's opinion of him, especially in the use of the adverb 'very', which sounds colloquial. If,
as Mrs Kernan hopes, the plot is to rehabilitate her husband, then
its success is uncertain. Martin Cunningham has been a resounding failure at rehabilitating his wife; he is worthy but ineffectual
and this may imply that, as with Mrs Cunningham, he will in the
long term fail again.

In Mrs Kernan, Joyce gives us a sober picture of a Dublin
woman's married life. She is described as an 'active, practical
woman of middle age' [p. 155] but as early as three weeks after
their marriage she had found a wife's life 'irksome' [p. 155] and
later becomes distracted by motherhood and four children. The
monotony of her current life is summarised in the fact that she
'accepted his frequent intemperance as a part of the climate'
[p. 155]. Mr Kernan has ceased being violent to her and her frustration with him is hinted at in her satisfaction that the
'shortening of his tongue would not be a great deficit'. She is of
course loyal, devoted to him as well as to her children, possibly out
of fear but relieved by occasional memories of their past romance;
she recalls that, in the days of their courtship, Tom was a 'not
ungallant figure' [p. 155] and at the wedding his silk hat had,
again, represented an outward show of decorum and courtliness.
Such recollections act as a contrast to the present unvarnished
realities of married life, and Joyce is often concerned to show such
an opposition between romanticised love and married life (for examples in *Dubliners*, see 'A Little Cloud' and 'A Painful Case'). For
the Kernans, love's old sweet song has now faded and we learn
that, after a quarter of a century of married life, Mrs Kernan 'had
few illusions left'.

This scepticism about married life extends also to the role of
religion in the prosaic lives of ordinary Dublin citizens, facing the

daily crises and dramas of their existence. Mrs Kernan accepts it of course: 'religion was religion', a fact of life for the average Dubliner, but she has few illusions left here, too, and religion has become a habit. By this I think the narrator means conventional religion; that is, church-going and all the trappings of the Church are empty of any deeply held commitment. Her faith in the Holy Ghost seems sustained by the same sort of superstition that could support the banshee (a female spirit whose cry portends an imminent death). Her level-headed kitchen- sink attitude to married life extends to religion and she regards the Sacred Heart as the most generally useful of her objects of devotion and she 'approves' of the sacraments. She sees Powers's religious plot as a very useful means to lever her husband back onto the tracks, which suggests that she considers religion as a means to an end rather than an end in itself.

The same utilitarian attitude to religion inspires Tom Kernan. He is a convert to Catholicism, a nominal Catholic, for reasons of his marriage, and by a process of simple arithmetic we can see that his faith lasted for only five years after the marriage. In fact, far from paying even lip-service to the Church he is fond of 'giving side-thrusts' at it; he is a doubting Thomas who despises the Jesuits as well as the ornamentation of the Catholic Church (such as the candles [p. 171]). Yet, in spite of this hatred, he is prepared to compromise his principles for commercial ends and this marks him out as a simoniac, selling his soul for secular advantage. On the whole, for most of the main characters here religion is not an end in itself, springing from a deep spiritual commitment, but merely a means to an end, and Joyce's point is that this is a form of simony, the use of divine grace for worldly ends. Mr Kernan in particular is ready to compromise for the sake of decorum and his standing in the business community. That his religious conviction is simply lukewarm is revealed not only in his initial conversion and subsequent lapse, but also in his ready acquiescence to the bedside inquisition of his respectable friends.

The conclusion to the story is a confirmation of this readiness to conform, revealed by Mr Kernan's appearance with a host of other Dublin businessmen in the Jesuit Church, 'all well dressed and orderly', and, in spite of his scorn for the Jesuits, he is 'sensible of the decorous atmosphere' [pp. 171–2]. With its slightly sardonic image of paradise, at least an earthly paradise, the final scene is the denouement of the gentlemen's plot, an indictment of the simony of Thomas Kernan and, by extension, of the general religious life of Dublin. Religious respectability is itself, like the silk hat, an essential appurtenance of the businessman.

(6) Select a fifth passage for discussion

The final page of 'The Dead' is Joyce's triumphant climax to *Dubliners*, a climax of intense feeling, even as Gabriel Conroy's consciousness begins to fade. The following passage occurs at the end of 'The Dead' where, in a Dublin hotel, Gabriel is falling asleep amid memories of the Morkans' party from which he and his wife, Gretta, have just returned.

> The air of the room chilled his shoulders. He stretched himself cautiously along under the sheets and lay down beside his wife. One by one they were all becoming shades. Better pass boldly into that other world, in the full glory of some passion, than fade and wither dismally with age. He thought of how she who lay beside him had locked in her heart for so many years that image of her lover's eyes when he had told her that he did not wish to live.
>
> Generous tears filled Gabriel's eyes. He had never felt like that himself towards any woman but he knew that such a feeling must be love. The tears gathered more thickly in his eyes and in the partial darkness he imagined he saw the form of a young man standing under a dripping tree. Other forms were near. His soul had approached that region where dwell the vast hosts of the dead. He was conscious of, but could not apprehend, their wayward and flickering existence. His own identity was fading out into a grey impalpable world: the solid world itself which these dead had one time reared and lived in was dissolving and dwindling.
>
> A few light taps upon the pane made him turn to the window. It had begun to snow again. He watched sleepily the flakes, silver and dark, falling obliquely against the lamplight. The time had come for him to set out on his journey westward. Yes, the newspapers were right: snow was general all over Ireland. It was falling on every part of the dark central plain, on the treeless hills, falling softly upon the Bog of Allen and, farther westward, softly falling into the dark mutinous Shannon waves. It was falling, too, upon every part of the lonely churchyard on the hill where Michael Furey lay buried. It lay thickly drifted on the crooked crosses and headstones, on the spears of the little gate, on the barren thorns. His soul swooned slowly as he heard the snow falling faintly through the universe and faintly falling, like the descent of their last end, upon all the living and the dead.
>
> [pp. 224–5]

Gabriel Conroy is alone again, within his thoughts. Even when he is at the party he feels and effectively appears to be alone, within his thoughts, often longing to escape to the snow-covered Phoenix Park, across the road from the Morkans' house. This sense of isolation is increased by Joyce's narrative method in the story, almost the whole of which issues through Gabriel's highly reflective and sensitive consciousness, which, together with his anxious personality, sets him apart and distant from the events of the party. We can see this here, above, too: sounds, actions and people have been progressively pared away until he is seen alone within his thought-tormented mind.

He has been crushed by Gretta's unexpected reminiscence of Michael Furey, a former lover, whose apparently selfless death and platonic devotion to her has acted as a bitter contrast to Gabriel's growing passion for his wife on their way back to the hotel room. The cold air, too, contrasts with Gabriel's passion, chilling his shoulders, a reminder of the moment when he arrived at the Morkan's house-party with snow 'like a cape on the shoulders of his overcoat' [p. 177].

The use of contrasts is an important feature of each of Joyce's works, helping to focus attention vividly on their themes and characters under consideration, and, in the above passage, we can examine how the use of such contrast operates. For example, Gabriel himself focuses on the tensions of life and death, the conscious and unconscious, internal and external settings. He stretches himself 'cautiously' and then he contemplates the opposite notion of passing 'boldly' into that other world. Similarly, in the same breath, he contrasts the 'full glory of some passion' with the idea of 'fade and wither dismally with age'. Out of these two contrasts there emerges, instead of the intended actions, an inertia which exactly matches and expresses Gabriel's incertitude, a feature which has dominated him throughout the story. And then the thought of Gretta's secret, locked away through the years of their marriage, exposes how much the revelation has undermined his self-esteem in relation to Gretta's feelings. Paralysed within this inertia Gabriel finds relief in a sort of parody of the death of Michael Furey in his own fading consciousness.

Into this paralysis Joyce brilliantly weaves opposing worlds of life and shade as Gabriel's consciousness slips into the twilight margins between wake and sleep, and life and death. The attention of the narrator (almost always adopting the point of view of Gabriel himself) focuses intensively at first on the eye, with the 'lover's eyes', taken up in the next sentence when Gabriel's own eyes fill with 'Generous tears' (Gretta has also previously described Gabriel as 'generous' [p. 219]) and the thickening tears create a literally darkening vision as well as the idea of melting, taken up later.

As he fades into his complex continent of sadness, guilt, disappointment and betrayal, the dissolving of his solid flesh into the 'grey impalpable world' offers him peace at last, a more satisfying escape from the reality which has continually tortured his thoughts during the evening, lightened only in brief interludes. The precise moment when consciousness begins to fade is signalled by the increasingly rhetorical tone of the narrator's language which parallels Gabriel's transition from the real, literal world into a metaphorical death, in 'that region where dwell the vast hosts of the dead' (in the second paragraph), while their 'wayward and flickering existence' expresses Gabriel's own irresolute state of mind. This desire – for another world – creates one aspect of the story's outward vision beyond the here and now, beyond self, Dublin and Ireland, beyond the unbearable reality and ache of longing, both of which Gabriel has continually experienced but only now fully expressed.

This is taken up and extended in the final paragraph as the attention switches more precisely beyond to the snows over Ireland, softening and concealing, leaving Gabriel disembodied, until it connects with Michael Furey's putative grave and its striking imagery of crosses, spears and thorns, briefly, unexpectedly evoking Christ and the idea of sacrifice. And then the idea dissolves beneath the soft fall of rhythmic sounds.

The mood of tranquil resignation and an atmosphere of dissolving are probably the first points to strike us about the above passage. This hypnotic shading off, not just of Gabriel's consciousness but also of his will and his point of view, highlights one of the narrative's key features: Gabriel's objectivity, his distance from people and events, which leaves the unmistakable impression that he is not a willing participant but a disengaged observer at life's feast. He has been nervous for almost the whole of the evening, starting with the aunts' anxiety over his arrival, and Lily, too, reminds him that he is late. He has unsettling encounters with some of the women and is made to confront his Irish past, almost as if he were a metaphor of national identity, which is ironic since, on the whole, he feels alienated from the rest of the party by his culture as well as by his intellect; for instance, he worries if his speech might not be understood by the others and he agonises over whether to leave out the Browning quotation – on the grounds that it would be 'above the heads of his hearers' [p. 179]; in fact, as if to confirm this Aunt Julia misses the point about his reference to the Three Graces).

To his aunts, Gabriel's solicitude is a 'standing joke' [p. 180]. He is a worrier, continually monitoring situations and his position in them, and because most of the story is told from Gabriel's point of view, it is permeated by an almost ever-present air of nervousness, tormenting its surface. Only now, as consciousness melts, 'dissolving and dwindling', does tranquillity begin to invade. Death is here for Gabriel a promise of release from the torment of his troubled universe.

This solicitude or oversensitivity of Gabriel's is revealed in the above passage in terms of his self-recrimination concerning love. Having just lusted after Gretta, his wife, her memory of Michael Furey has caused an abrupt reversal of Gabriel's increasing passion, and his solicitude becomes translated into self-persecution and guilt. There is no sense of jealousy, only self-recrimination at his own perceived deficiency in comparison to Michael Furey's apparently noble self-sacrifice.

So his solicitude also leads him, as a result of these unbearable emotions, to seek escape – to seek solitude amid the deathly paralysing snow which is 'general all over Ireland' (in reality he will be driven abroad by what Ireland represents – the trap of the past). But is Gabriel justified in the conclusions which lead him this way, as he begins to fall asleep? Gretta's story is a moving one and thematically it reiterates the story's concern with the themes of generosity and hospitality, which Gabriel's after-dinner speech has set out. In particular, it helps to sketch out the Christian elements of the narrative – especially appropriate as the story is set sometime during the Christmas period (the most likely setting is the feast of the Epiphany). At the same time, Joyce places these hints of Christmas alongside ironic hints of the agony of the crucifixion, in the references to crosses, spears and thorns in the final paragraph. Gabriel experiences his own agony after a last supper in which his accuser, Molly Ivors, betrays and then leaves him. Note also the references to selflessness or doing things for others, and charity: Mount Melleray [p. 201] and the generosity of the Misses Morkan, Gabriel giving money to Lily, paying the cabman, and being repaid by Freddy Malins who also runs out into the cold night to find cabs for everyone – there is a general air of goodwill.

Set against this are examples of selfishness, for example Mr

Browne's ungracious attitude to the monks, and he continually tries to score off Freddy Malins (who is the soul of friendship as well as of the party); there is also the Pope's ungrateful treatment of the women choristers [p. 195], and the unseasonal attacks from Lilly and Molly Ivors. Added to this is insincerity – in the empty gesture of applauding Mary Jane's piano playing and of Gabriel's hypocrisy about his aunts as 'two ignorant old women' [p. 193].

So the climax to these two opposing strands, of hospitality and ingratitude, is reached in Gretta's story about Michael Furey. Gabriel implicitly interprets the relationship of Gretta and Michael in idealised, chastely platonic terms as a foil to his own lust-driven yearning for Gretta. In any event, he feels deeply humbled by her account, 'He had never felt like that himself towards any woman but he knew that such a feeling must be love' [p. 224]. But, we may ask, a feeling like what? On the previous page to this he reflects that 'a man had died for her sake' [p. 223], but did Michael Furey die for the motive that Gabriel ascribes to him? Or is Gabriel confused by his own solicitude? In fact, Furey did not really die as a self-sacrifice in the Christian sense or for any positive purpose at all. The phrase 'for her sake' can equally be interpreted as 'on account of her' (although Gabriel does not, of course, see it this way). Although at first sight Michael Furey's death appears to symbolise the general theme of selfless charity which runs through the story – death as a sacrifice – this is illusory. He does not die out of love but out of something negative and probably obsessive such as infatuation, as far as we can tell anyway (we have, of course, only Gretta's version). His death is an idle waste and negative, and it serves principally as a further instance of the way in which the dead cling to the living as another form of paralysis.

But Gabriel's solicitude makes him an unreliable narrator, and his versions of himself and others is uncertain. The crucial point here is that, as the story has shown and the final paragraph confirms, it is Gabriel who represents mature love, and although Gabriel's words for Michael Furey suggest some Christ-like sacrifice, it is Gabriel who has the Christian consciousness and conscience, as well as the ability to make sense of what happens even at the cost of his own distress.

And who are the dead of the title? As we read 'The Dead' we are constantly being reminded of death in a variety of ways: in the memories of those who have died, in the deathlike descriptions of the people at the party (Lily is 'pale', Julia 'grey', Freddy 'pallid', Kate 'shrivelled' and Browne is 'wizzened'), in the imminence of future deaths (in Gabriel's thoughts), and in the name 'Lily', the flower often associated with the dead. So the story gives us two levels of the dead: the deceased (such as Ellen, Gabriel's mother, Pat, her brother, and Michael Furey) and the living dead, which include Mr Browne, Lily, Mrs Malins and those others of Dublin who inhabit a moribund existence. But what of Gabriel? How does he fit into this realm of the dead? Some critics have suggested that the 'dead' in the title include Gabriel, on the grounds that the final page hints at his slow descent into a death-like unconsciousness and even that he willingly embraces its oblivion (they cite the reference to the snow on Gabriel's shoulders as he enters the party). At the same time, the party has affinities with hell, not least for its harrowing of souls including Gabriel's, and there is an impish image of Freddy Malins waving his devilish fork at the close of Gabriel's speech [p. 207]. It is as though the soul of Gabriel had entered hell: on the final page, 'His soul had approached that region where dwell the vast hosts of the dead'. There are other suggestions that Gabriel is the dead, not least in his request for the supper guests to 'kindly forget my existence' [p. 199] – although, as the story reveals, no one can forget the existence of the dead, let alone the living.

However, other critics have interpreted the ending as metaphorical death, a vision of death in life, and I would favour this interpretation. Although the final passage focuses closely on Gabriel's self-mortifying solicitude, it really does not presage his death. Instead, by plummeting these depths, Gabriel is permitted to come to terms with his wife's stunning revelation. In fact the memory of the dead Michael Furey is a vivid demonstration of the paralysing effect of the dead upon the living, and one of many memories of the deceased occurring throughout, chiefly but not exclusively in Gabriel's thoughts; for instance, there is the memory of Gabriel's dead mother, Ellen, sister of Kate and Julia (although little is mentioned of his father 'T.J.'); dinner talk leads to memories of dead opera singers; there is the dead grandfather, Patrick Morkan, and his dead horse, Johnny (ironically condemned to walk in paralysed circles at the glue or starch mill, haunted by the bones of dead horses [pp. 208–9]); the monks in their coffins at Mount Melleray constantly remind themselves of their 'last end' in their *memento mori* coffins; and there are memo-

ries of the past, of Gabriel's and Gretta's childhoods, of the salad
days of the Morkan sisters and of the golden age of Irish hospitality recalled with other memories by Gabriel in his after-dinner
speech.

Gabriel's speech, as well as setting the keynote theme of Irish
hospitality, makes explicit this theme of the ever-undying dead
who clutch and cling to the living, who either will not let go or
who are not released by the living:

> the memory of those dead and gone great ones whose fame the world will not
> willingly let die.
>
> [p. 204].

So, at the close of the story, when Gabriel reflects on how they
are becoming shades [pp. 224–5] he undergoes a metaphorical
death in that the dead, in clinging to the living, draw the life from
them, pulling them down into a kind of purgatory, between the
two states, and it is to this that Gabriel succumbs. Rather than a
literal vision of his actual death, the final passage is a dire warn-
ing of the death of the spirit at the hands of the ghosts of the past
who inhabit (and inhibit) the life of the living.

(7) Have I achieved a sufficiently complex sense of the text?

It is difficult to say 'yes' to this question simply on the basis of the
passages from the five stories we have so far considered. We can
say that we have begun to appreciate the variety of methods
and concerns in the collection, but to understand the subtlety of
Joyce's achievement in this work we will need to examine more
of the stories. We have seen how a diverse group of characters have
encountered crises of life and death and how these crises have
reflected on them, particularly as they became aware of themselves, as in the cases of James Duffy and Gabriel Conroy. Our
analysis has revealed, too, the often deep sensitivity of Joyce's
people and the way these sensitivities contribute to their suffering;
the boy in 'The Sisters' and Eveline come to mind here as well as
Gabriel again, in 'The Dead'. At the same time Joyce has presented
an indicting picture of the city of Dublin as a prison house,
plagued both by desire and inertia, which are also important
factors in the creation of Joyce's comic effect. We have gained an
insight into the frustrations and internal pressures of urban exist-

ence, via its people, while also noting some of the superhuman forces at work in the city. Also, through our examination of the city and its people, we have seen how important a study of Joyce's subtle use of language can be to an appreciation of his overall effect: at the centre of any study of Joyce there must be a detailed study of his language, and we will address ourselves to this in the next stage of our discussion.

Our examination of a selection of stories has treated them in isolation by and large, and in doing so it is easy to overlook one of the key elements in Joyce's creation of meaning, and that is the unity of his text. The stories were not, finally, intended to be understood in isolation from each other because their fuller meanings are created by reference across and through the stories of the whole collection. Through their 'intertextuality', meanings arise and cumulate, become modified, re-viewed and revised, and to appreciate anything of the complexity of the work we should consider the stories as an integrated whole.

One of the most apparent of the elements which help to integrate the stories is the city of Dublin itself, and indeed the city emerges distinctly as a character in its own right, single in its plurality. The malaise of the city is encountered again and again: its citizens are continually encountering common predicaments in their public lives and, most importantly, within themselves, as a result of their citizenship (even when they choose to ignore it). Moreover, we can see that their encounters frequently have identical spiritual consequences.

The conception of the city as a trap is not difficult for us to recognise here. Yet we may also become aware at the same time of a dichotomy in that the people of the book are both the instigators as well as the victims of the trap. James Duffy is the epitome of this dichotomy. As we have seen, he abjures the city 'of which he was a citizen' and then he undergoes the painful process of understanding the extent of his moral vacuity: as a citizen who denies the spiritual life of the community he contributes to the very malady he scorns. 'A Painful Case' is one of the book's most moving portrayals of the profound awareness of the guilt and angst lurking beneath the surface of Dublin city life.

In each of the stories, we come away with an acute feeling of having understood the soul of its characters, which is a feeling usually limited to longer, novelistic works of literature. And yet what Joyce works on here are but some few subtle brushworks of impressionistic intensity. As we have begun to see, I hope, Joyce's method is one of compelling economy and, while we have made a start on examining the techniques in the collection, we will need to go deeper and observe them in action in further contexts. Therefore, in the second part of this chapter we can continue by examining in detail the aspects which help to unify this collection of stories.

II Aspects of the text

A simple way of working out the features which unite the stories of *Dubliners* is to consider what they have in common – for instance, backgrounds and foregrounds, recurring ideas, characters and situations, and Joyce's methods of portraying them, especially his use of language. With this in mind, my approach in this part of our analysis is first to trace some of the unifying features in the book, and then to try to build a fuller interpretation on these by examining some of the other stories not yet considered.

To begin with, most of the central characters in the five stories are quite lonely figures, often in spite of the communal life of Dublin in which they are immersed. The small boy in 'The Sisters' feels alienated firstly by the fuddled mentality of the adults such as old Cotter who misunderstand and then patronise him, and secondly by the death of his mentor Father Flynn whose absence continues to exert a sombre force on the boy's thoughts. Eveline is equally isolated but by the dilemma of her divided loyalties: to her family, to Frank and lastly to herself. James Duffy, in 'A Painful Case', is isolated both physically by his self-imposed exile on the outskirts of Dublin ('as far as possible from the city of which he was a citizen' [p. 103]) and spiritually by his equally self-imposed emotional separation. Where Mr Duffy can be described as a self-made isolationist, Eveline is separated from other people by the very drive to connect with them. And, as we have seen already, although Gabriel socialises at the Morkan's party he is really in a party for the dead, a ghost sonata in which he becomes isolated from the vital life. He becomes a victim of, on the one hand, his own fears and, on the other, the clutches of the living dead. In fact, in the stories so far considered, only Tom Kernan can be said to enjoy a gregarious existence, although his gregariousness can be viewed as an adjunct to his readiness to conform, to submit to the decorum of respectable society and religion.

Another important aspect of *Dubliners* which you may already have experienced is the degree of uncertainty they feature. It is not usually possible to fix Joyce's intentions in these stories or to reduce them to a single, absolute interpretation. The stories are ambivalent and the chief reason for this is Joyce's silence. Although silence is a strong feature of all his works, it is most evident here in *Dubliners* where he often omits information which would make meanings explicit. His use of silence as a stratagem is signalled in the first paragraph of the book, as we have seen, by the reference to the 'gnomon', a geometric figure in which a part is missing. In each of the stories there is always something important missing or silent. Ironically, Joyce's silences occur in spite of the fact that on the material level he often appears to go out of his way to provide minutely detailed information.

Some examples should help to make this clearer. On a simple level, we never discover the name of the boy in the opening stories (the first-person narrator who also appears in 'An Encounter' and in 'Araby') or the name of Mangan's sister, while in 'Eveline' Joyce stops abruptly short of revealing whether Eveline does escape with Frank, a point which exactly hits at the dilemma of her situation. In 'Grace', mystery surrounds the young cyclist who rescues Tom Kernan, as it surrounds Kernan himself in the early part of the story. And in 'The Dead' we learn hardly anything of Gabriel Conroy's background: what does he do? how old is he (which is important to the story's theme of time)? and what was the Browning quotation which he decides to omit?

Equally, stories frequently begin silently in *medias res* and usually end suddenly in an abrupt silence. That such silences are a deliberate strategy is clear from the way that at other times Joyce focuses on details quite intensely; for example, we are given the exact date and place of Father Flynn's death in 'The Sisters', the name of the opera which Frank took Eveline to see, a detailed newspaper report of Mrs Sinico's death, and, in 'The Dead', there is precise attention to details such as facial appearances and the lavish spread on the dinner table. Such precision is all one with Joyce's characteristic use of authenticating documents (such as funeral cards, song lyrics, letters, newspaper reports, poems and canvassing cards) and of materialistic realism in the form of actual and precise Dublin locations (often using the names of real Dubliners). Such detail acts as a foil to Joyce's silences, which manipulate us by raising and dashing our expectations, drawing us into the text to try to discover information and to encourage us to reshape its details and construct our own meanings.

Joyce's technique of focusing-in on details is, of course, important in providing the surface material of his text, but it is also a key device in revealing the nature of characters' inner states. This is suggested, too, in Joyce's use of the term 'epiphany' to describe such moments of intensity and revelation. We can see that almost every one of the *Dubliners* stories is structured around such an epiphany as its climax; for example, Eveline realises truths about her home (though not about herself), while James Duffy becomes vividly aware of his vanity and his poverty of spirit. Typically, in such moments, characters are isolated from their immediate environment, with their attention focused inwards, encapsulated in silence, a silence that helps to point up both their isolation and sudden self-awareness. And the silence of such epiphanies often reverberates with moral energy beyond the close of a story so that it acts as a form of ironic statement on what has happened.

At the same time, you may have noticed how Joyce is careful never to intrude his authorial voice into the narrative; he never passes a moral comment on characters, at least not directly, but tries to remain outside or beyond what is happening. On the face of it, it might appear to be difficult to narrate a story without the author giving explicit moral guidance to the reader, which is the case in most conventional narratives. But Joyce does not envisage his role as a moral guide to the reader and his moral position within the narrative is never explicitly defined. So how does Joyce tell the story if he adopts these attitudes of silence? If we look closely we can see that he does this efficiently and pragmatically by arranging the story to filter through the eyes of the central character. By adopting the point of view of the character, Joyce allows the events to take on a natural appearance since not only are they portrayed through the character of the observer-narrator (and in the process revealing important elements of the observer's personality), but events and descriptions also appear to be selected and ordered quite logically by the observer's consciousness.

For this reason the events in Joyce's works rarely occur in chronological sequence but usually involve flashbacks and leaps forward. 'Eveline' is an ideal example of this since although the story covers in time perhaps only one hour and, possibly, only one place (if we allow that the tailpiece at the docks may take place only in Eveline's imagination), Eveline's consciousness continually switches from the present to the past, from her sitting room window to her shop, to the theatre, a picnic on the Hill of Howth and even to Canada and Buenos Aires; yet nowhere does Joyce make any comment on her. Another advantage lies in the fact that, in adopting the point of view of the character, Joyce often (though not always) creates a source of insight and empathy for the character, and consequently sympathy, as in the case of Eveline.

This technique, now usually called 'free indirect style', reaches maturity in A Portrait. It is a form of third-person narration which adopts the vocabulary and idiom of a character in order to convey his or her personality and view. It has the significant advantage of enabling a narrative to appear to arise naturally through the perspective of a character who becomes both an actor and a narrator and, further, a commentator on him/herself as well as on the action, thus making a moral point of view still possible. And the device of the epiphany is an effective element here in making explicit meanings intelligible, once again through a character's point of view. So, at the end of 'A Painful Case' James Duffy rebukes himself as 'outcast from life's feast', and in the accusing darkness he becomes terrifyingly aware of his moral bankruptcy. As we have seen in 'The Dead', too, Gabriel Conroy reproaches himself for what he regards as his failure of love and a general spiritual hollowness.

If we look at a more detailed example, Joyce's device should be easier to understand. In the closing pages of 'A Little Cloud' we see Little Chandler intensely humiliated by the heroicised image of his old associate Ignatius Gallaher, whose bachelor life as a foreign journalist seems a rakish adventure compared to his own timid existence in a legal office. In fact Gallaher's is an image very much of Chandler's own making, a projection of his own stunted ambitions rather than a reality. It is only a version of the man and so the projection (which Gallaher is happy to encourage) effectively acts to define Chandler's unhappy lot. He is a small man, introverted and overscrupulous, who nurses half-hearted hopes rather than valid expectations, and his continual moralising to Gallaher seeks to compensate for his own patent inadequacies.

Towards the end of the story we see him alone, having returned home from his reunion, reflecting on the meanness of his own life through the eyes of his wife, Annie, in her photograph. It is an epiphany not unlike that of Eveline's and both characters share a similar domestic frustration, an inability to seize the moment, a want of enterprise.

> He looked coldly into the eyes of the photograph and they answered coldly. Certainly they were pretty and the face itself was pretty. But he found something mean in it. Why was it so unconscious and ladylike? The composure of the eyes irritated him. They repelled him and defied him: there was no passion in them, no rapture. He thought of what Gallaher had said about rich Jewesses. Those dark Oriental eyes, he thought, how full they are of passion, of voluptuous longing! . . . Why had he married the eyes in the photograph?
>
> [p. 78]

This passage is fairly typical of Joyce's style in *Dubliners* and we can use it to examine how the narrator uses a changing point of view for different effects. The opening sentence begins with an objective statement in which the narrator tries to make the language refer to a realistic setting, although the repeated word 'coldly' hints at the moral tone which follows. With the adverb 'Certainly' the point of view switches to that of Chandler, and then the repeated weak adjective 'pretty' takes up Annie's own earlier description of a blouse, an event recalled now by Chandler, revealing how it still works on his sensitivity. Similarly, although the questions seem at first to be those of the narrator they are of course Chandler's, expressing his mounting frustration with life, regarding his marriage now as an impasse. This reaches a climax on the following page:

> *It was useless. He couldn't read. He couldn't do anything.* The wailing of the child pierced the drum of his ear. *It was useless, useless! He was a prisoner for life.* His arms trembled with anger and suddenly bending to the child's face he shouted:
> – Stop!
>
> [pp. 79–80]

I have emphasised here the parts which seem to me to be in free indirect style, expressing through Chandler's eyes his own inner discourse. The insistent word 'useless' throbs in his mind, taking up his own use of the word at the beginning of the story: 'he felt how useless it was to struggle against fortune' [p. 66]. But by the end of the story the epithet has gathered up other related words referring to Chandler himself or to Dublin, such as disillusioned, melancholy, shyness, fear, dust, decrepit, nothing, little. Dublin is several times the object of his frustration but in reality this is only an outward reflex, a denial of his own weaknesses, and he timidly submits to what he calls 'fortune'.

Notice how the narrator cleverly avoids making a direct moral comment on Chandler, leaving him instead to make it himself. The result is doubly effective. We become more intimate with the character's consciousness at this crucial moment but, further, by adopting this internal state within the fraught mind of Chandler we get a clearer idea of his frustration, especially in the obsessive recurrence of Chandler's words and his unresolved self-examination, which turns him back onto his distressed consciousness.

Another way in which Joyce creates implicit moral meanings while maintaining silence is through symbolism. Joyce usually draws attention to his symbols through the use of silence, making them stand out as intense details yet at the same time attaching them mystically to their contexts. There are many examples but they include the chalice in 'The Sisters', a rotting apple in 'A Painful Case', Tom Kernan's silk hat, the Morkans' horse, and the snow at the end of 'The Dead'.

Sense impressions, especially of colours and odours, are usually precise and significant, with a precision deriving from Joyce's verbal dexterity as well as from his powers of observation. His frequent use of the colours yellow and brown is almost always symbolic, underlining the theme of stagnation and paralysis in the lives of Dubliners, and other motifs which recur through the collection have a symbolic edge; for example, movement is usually associated with unrest (and is often circular), coins suggest trade and domination (of human lives), while the word 'confused' is frequently a euphemism for sexual excitement or arousal. The two labels 'little' and 'heavy' almost invariably indicate a mean and adventureless life.

We can study Joyce's symbolism in action by taking a close look at the following, a passage from 'Araby':

> The former tenant of our house, a priest, had died in the back drawing-room. Air, musty from having been long enclosed, hung in all the rooms, and the waste room behind the kitchen was littered with old useless papers. Among these I found a few paper-covered books, the pages of which were curled and damp: *The Abbott* by Walter Scott, *The Devout Communicant* and *The Memoirs of Vidocq*. I liked the last best because its leaves were yellow. The wild garden behind the house contained a central apple-tree and a few straggling bushes under one of which I found the late tenant's rusty bicycle-pump. He had been a very charitable priest; in his will he had left all his money to institutions and the furniture of his house

to his sister.

When the short days of winter came dusk fell before we had well eaten our dinners. When we met in the street the house had grown sombre. The space of the sky above us was the colour of ever-changing violet and towards it the lamps of the street lifted their feeble lanterns. The cold air stung us and we played till our bodies glowed. Our shout echoed in the silent street. The career of our play brought us through the dark muddy lanes behind the houses where we ran the gauntlet of the rough tribes from the cottages, to the back doors of the dark dripping gardens where odours arose from the ashpits, to the dark odorous stables where the coachman smoothed and combed the horse or shook music from the buckled harness. When we returned to the street light from the kitchen windows had filled the areas. If my uncle was seen turning the corner we hid in the shadow until we had seen him safely housed. Or if Mangan's sister came out on the doorstep to call her brother in for his tea we watched her from our shadow peer up and down the street. We waited to see whether she would remain or go in and, if she remained, we left our shadow and walked up to Mangan's steps resignedly. She was waiting for us, her figure defined by the light from the half-opened door. Her brother always teased her before he obeyed and I stood by the railings looking at her. Her dress swung as she moved her body and the soft rope of her hair tossed from side-to-side.

[pp. 21–2]

One important point about Joyce's writing is how his language operates so readily on the symbolic level as well as on the literal level. For instance, this passage presents a realistic, lyrical description of the boy's energetic life at home and play in its closely observed details – the room behind the kitchen, books, an apple-tree, a bicycle pump, the dark evening streets. And yet Joyce's selection of these diverse elements offers them up for our particular consideration and we have come to learn that such details in Joyce more often than not have a symbolic charge to them. We might for, instance, relate the statement 'a priest had died' here with the death of Father Flynn in 'The Sisters', and its hints of the decline of religion, while the 'musty' air anticipates the 'odour of cretonne' at the start of 'Eveline' and its overtones of stifling decay. And Joyce's choice of epithets here indicates the curve of a decline: waste, useless, damp, yellow, rusty – they become a familiar, sad complement to Dublin lives.

Equally, Joyce's choice of books found in the garden turn out to be revealingly coherent with the themes of the story. *The Abbott* concerns another boy-hero, a dedicated page to Mary Queen of Scots, *The Devout Communicant* points in the same direction, of a pious acolyte, while *The Memoirs of Vidocq* concern a cunning French undercover agent. The three ideas converge two pages later when the boy, nursing secret longings for Mangan's sister, conceives himself in heroic terms, as bearing his chalice 'safely through a throng of foes' [p. 23], seeing himself in the guise of a priest in the times of persecution (in contrast with the departed owner of the rusty bicycle pump). Again and again we are invited by Joyce to explore in depth such details as the titles of books and songs, and the rewards repay the effort required.

In the second paragraph of the above extract from 'Araby' we can note how Joyce sustains the theme of childhood secrecy in his brilliant evocation of the evening world of games, played out beneath a cloak of darkness and silence. It vividly sets up the alternative, other world of childhood set apart from adults, which has been peopled by such unromantic figures as old Cotter, the stranger in 'An Encounter', and the boy's uncle here in 'Araby'. The repetition of 'dark' and 'shadow' underpin this subculture of tribal loyalties and secrecy, and with the appearance of Mangan's sister we are immediately brought to the symbolic possibilities of the play of dark and light. Her body is defined by the light from a 'half-opened door' and she appears as a saintly vision in stark silhouette, a vision which enunciates both the sensuality and the sanctity of her body. We can recognise in the moment of the vision the awakening of sexuality in the boy, while his frustrated mission to the 'Araby' bazaar operates as a correlative of his sexual frustrations.

The sexual theme has been hinted earlier with the reference to the 'central apple-tree' in the garden (and its hint of an Eden-like failure) and the fact of her door being 'half-opened' endorses her as a figure of seduction, beckoning like the exotic promise of the bazaar itself ('The syllables of the word "Araby" were called to me through the silence in which my soul luxuriated and cast an eastern enchantment over me' [p. 24]). While darkness has become linked with childhood, the light of Mangan's sister becomes linked with adulthood. Yet light is also traditionally connected with Mary, the Virgin, and we can note that the boy's awakening feelings become confused and diverted into a sort of cultic devotion to the Virginal girl. She is prevented from accompanying him to the bazaar by a retreat at her convent and this additional frustration turns him into a devoted page for her distant, idealised image (uniting the earlier idea of Mary, Queen of Scots, and the Virgin into one). In his desire she becomes for him an icon of devotion, an idea rather than an attainable reality. Her idealisation is underlined by the point that for us she remains unnamed, in spite of the fact that 'her name sprang to my lips at moments in strange prayers and praises' [p. 23] – though perhaps we can guess with some confidence that her name is Mary. His crusade-like quest to the eastern bazaar of Araby founders, in the realisation of the emptiness of his romantic idealism, and the moment is a foretaste of what becomes a familiar emotional cadence in the lives of older Dubliners. As elsewhere, while the symbolism of the story sets up the reader's expectations in it, it ultimately works against the character's own explicit ideals (which nevertheless help to sustain the story's interest), and by the end of 'Araby' we can see how the symbolism of failure and waste eventually comes to dominate and he is dashed by them. The sense of failure provokes our emotional response but less by its particular impact on this small boy than by its capacity to become a habitual resonance in the collection.

The characters we have looked at so far have been principally male, but how does Joyce portray women in *Dubliners*? Well, like Mangan's sister they are often both figures of seduction and yet of virginal elusiveness; and, in addition, as in, say, Eveline's case, they often have the symbolic role of the mother. Joyce's woman in *Dubliners* is most often seen as the drudge, holding the home and the family together. For example, in 'The Sisters', Nannie and Eliza conduct the practical business after the death of their crazy brother priest, and Eveline's dream of escape is from the excessive duty to the family home, a life of 'hard work to keep the house together'; other examples of the cheerless drudge in the collection are Maria in 'Clay', Mrs Kernan in 'Grace' and the girl in 'Two Gallants'. For Mrs Sinico in 'A Painful Case', part of her tragedy is not merely that she dies in an unpleasant accident but that in emulating the drink-ridden archetype of Dublin man she is guilty of abandoning the conventional role of mother-skivvy – and Mr Duffy is repelled by this neglect. Mrs Kernan had hoped for escape from the 'unbearable' and 'irksome' life of a wife through motherhood, but now 'she had very few illusions left' [p. 156].

As individuals and types, women are both disenfranchised and impotent, the limits of their existence determined by man. They are repeatedly depicted as powerless, passive and silent. But there are deviations from this model. Mrs Mooney in 'A Boarding House' has separated from her husband with financial independence and is a manipulator of men. Mrs Kearney, in the ironically titled 'A Mother', reveals an unusual, if overdeveloped, drive to assert herself and discovers how this can be diverted and blunted by a male regime whose charge of 'I thought you were a lady [p. 147] sums up her refusal to conform to male expectations. Molly Ivors, in 'The Dead', remains the only genuine expression of free-woman in *Dubliners*, and Gabriel's fright at her treatment of him reveals his conventional expectations of her. She is anticipated in the same story by Lily, defined in male terms as 'the caretaker's daughter', whose rejection of Gabriel's coin [p. 178] symbolises her rejection of the male will. But Molly Ivors signifies a new type of woman. With an independence of mind, she is prepared to hassle Gabriel on her own political terms, and she disrupts his tranquil assumption of a quiet and compliant woman. She refuses to be pinned down and eventually escapes from the world of the dead with a sardonic flourish.

But such impulses of flight are rare in *Dubliners* for effectively there is no escape, for either sex. Bob Doran's inextricable situation in 'A Boarding House' is a good example. After indulging himself in Polly Mooney's flirtatious charms he slowly becomes aware that he has been ambushed, and only just before Mrs Mooney ('who dealt with moral problems as a cleaver deals with meat' [p. 58]) summons him downstairs:

All his long years of service gone for nothing! All his industry and diligence thrown away! As a young man he had sown his wild oats, of course; he had boasted of his free-thinking and denied the existence of God to his companions in public-houses. But that was all past and done with . . . nearly. He still bought a copy of *Reynolds Newspaper* every week, but he attended to his religious duties, and for nine-tenths of the year lived a regular life. He had money enough to settle down on; it was not that. But the family would look down on her. First of all there was her disreputable father, and then her mother's boarding house was beginning to get a certain fame. He had a notion that he was being had. He could imagine his friends talking of the affair and laughing. She *was* a little vulgar; sometimes she said *I seen* and *If I had've known*. But what would grammar matter if he really loved her? He could not make up his mind whether to like her or despise her for what she had done. Of course he had done it too. His instinct urged him to remain free, not to marry. Once you are married you are done for, it said.

While he was sitting helplessly on the side of the bed in shirt and trousers, she tapped lightly at his door and entered. She told him all, that she had made a clean breast of it to her mother and that her mother would speak with him that morning. She cried and threw her arms round his neck, saying:

– O Bob! Bob! What am I to do? What am I to do at all?'

She would put an end to herself, she said.

He comforted her feebly, telling her not to cry, that it would be all right, never fear. He felt against his shirt the agitation of her bosom.

It was not altogether his fault that it had happened. He remembered well, with the curious patient memory of the celibate, the first casual caresses her dress, her breath, her fingers had given him. Then late one night as he was undressing for bed she had tapped at his door, timidly. She wanted to relight her candle at his, for hers had been blown out by a gust. It was her bath night. She wore a loose open combing-jacket of printed flannel. Her white instep shone in the opening of her furry slippers and the blood glowed warmly behind her perfumed skin. From her hands and wrists too as she lit and steadied her candle a faint perfume arose.

[pp. 61–2]

The story has a good many comic ironies, although its exquisite silences make it unclear whether we ought to regard Bob Doran as a hapless victim or a helpless fool. And between the silences we have, instead of explicit information, gestures, signs and hints which we have to try to read if we are to make sense of this. It is not easy, for the characters of Polly and Mrs Mooney also appear distant and slightly turned from our view.

Does Bob fall or is he pushed? Joyce does not tell us. The above passage, though, is an epiphany in which Bob Doran becomes aware of the consequences of his actions, with his particular view of the events. He is trapped but he sees the trap in terms of his work and his family, and the shame which will spring from both sources, rather than in terms of his own will; even before he met Polly he was in thrall to these two forces. That he is compromised by his intimacy with Polly only adds an extra wall to the cell in which he now stews. This is ironically emphasised by his pretensions to free-thinking and the rest but, of course, he is only a part-time libertine – the most that can be aspired to in parochial Dublin.

His mind is a confused mixture of contradictions and he is unable now to see how exactly he got into this fix; he has a notion that 'he was being had' and he scorns Polly for what 'she had done'; but then he had done 'it' too and, a little later, 'It was not altogether his fault'. These fluctuations clearly represent Bob Doran's confused and tormented mind as well as his indignation at being had, although his pride will not allow him to reconcile the idea of being a free-thinker with his being compromised on all sides. He is torn between desire and loathing but, in spite of his pride, his thoughts lapse back into a recall of Polly's momentous visit, and his imagination indulges in a mildly sensuous fantasy of perfumed caresses with the unmistakable eroticism of her relight-

ing her candle against his. He is a victim of his own desires, but at
least his fantasy is one of the few places left for him to escape.

It is no accident, of course, that Bob and Polly meet and make
love, or so we infer. Mrs Mooney casts a cold scrutinous eye on all
the goings-on in the house and, because Polly is (euphemistically)
'very lively' she is given 'the run of the young men' [pp. 57–8] by
her mother, who is known as '*The Madam*' (and Bob reflects that
the house was 'beginning to get a certain fame'). There is thus
more than a hint that the boarding house resembles a 'bordello'
or brothel run by this implacable Madam who monitors the guests
to check if any of them 'meant business'. This is how love is con-
strued by the ex-butcher's wife in her hard, calculating world with
its thinly veiled regime of cunning and tyranny (even the sugar
and butter are 'under lock and key' [p. 59], policed by the grim
presence of Polly's brother Jack, who appears to have inherited his
father's talent for brutality.

In depicting match-making and marriage as a sort of con-trick
this story is a companion piece to 'Two Gallants', and comple-
ments the distorted image of love represented elsewhere in the
book where, like the spirit of the people, it becomes suppressed,
submerged and distorted and what we are shown (at least until
'The Dead') is only its unhealthy repercussions – for instance, in
'A Little Cloud' and 'A Painful Case'. The Mooneys' own marital
history is marked by its violent failure, and there are also echoes
of such failure in 'Counterparts'. In 'Grace', too, the failure of
love in marriage is depicted, but from the wife's point of view:
'After three weeks she had found a wife's life irksome . . . unbearable . . . ' [p. 155]. Such models act as a sombre precursor for Bob
as well as for the idealistic boy of 'Araby' and for Eveline: '[Frank]
would give her life, perhaps love too' [p. 33]. Dubliners marry for
many motives, but it would seem that love is not foremost among
them.

In simple terms Bob is trapped by the free expression of his
sexual drive, which in the world of Dublin really ought to have
been, like the sugar and the butter, locked up, but which is coaxed
by Polly's lively allure ('I'm a . . . naughty girl' [p. 57]); sex is taboo
and the silences and equivocations of the story play on this. Bob's
fear of Mrs Mooney's wrath (backed by the shadow of Jack's
violence) intensifies his gloom, already darkened by the fear of
the 'loss of his sit' [p. 60], since he is employed by a 'great Catholic'. He reflects that 'Dublin is such a small city: everyone knows

everyone else's business' [p. 61], and it dawns on him that he is in checkmate to the forces of the city's social, religious and economic constraints, so adroitly manipulated by Mrs Mooney.

The story ends with Bob's pretensions exposed and shattered, and his feebly optimistic 'Perhaps they could be happy . . . ' is undermined by the cold realism of his own reflection that, in Dublin at any rate, 'Once you are married you are done for . . . '. For Dubliners, marriage marks the end of experience, almost the end of hope, the archetypal trap (compare, for instance, the treatment of early married life in the next story, 'A Little Cloud' where Ignatius Gallaher describes it as putting your 'head in the sack' [p. 76]).

As we have seen, the Dubliners are trapped in a general paralysis more or less of their own making, but of which they rarely become aware, and the chief source of humour in the book is the inexhaustible capacity of characters for self-deception or self-delusion. Their ignorance of this is both a cause and an effect in the cycle of their dilemma. There is an incessant ebb of decline in the currents of these Dublin lives towards archetypal situations in which people continually fail, as the opening sentence of the book cheerlessly prefigures: 'There was no hope for him this time . . . '. Many lead lives of misery, as in the case of the Farringtons and the Chandlers, and almost every one of them has an 'adventureless tale' of hopelessness and half-hearted endeavour which collectively constitutes the tragedy of Dublin. In this way the city as a whole, in the form of its citizens, is itself a major character and the central object of Joyce's tragicomic vision.

In 'After the Race' Joyce mocks the Dubliners as the 'gratefully oppressed' [p. 35] on account both of their willing acceptance of their grim lot and their readiness to palliate its causes. His point in writing these stories was, in part, to reveal and confront the citizens of Dublin with their moral malaise as a first step to changing it, as he revealed in a letter to a close friend in 1904, during an early stage of the composition of *Dubliners*:

> I am writing a series of epicleti – ten – for a paper. I have written one. I call the series *Dubliners* to betray the soul of that hemiplegia or paralysis which many consider a city.

Although, at first, Joyce set out to write a series of essentially separate and unconnected stories, he later conceived of them, together with new stories, within a unified whole, structured through a progression of ages from youth to maturity, according to the ages of the principal characters in each, beginning with the young boy of the first three stories and ending with stories of adult public life ('Ivy Day', 'A Mother', 'Grace'):

> My intention was to write a chapter of the moral history of my country and I chose Dublin for the scene because that city seemed to me the centre of paralysis. I have tried to present it to the indifferent public under four of its aspects: childhood, adolescence, maturity and public life. The stories are arranged in this order. I have written it for the most part in a style of scrupulous meanness.

'The Dead' was added at a later date after Joyce considered that he had been too severe on his old home-town (although he never altered his conviction about the traps and paralyses of Dublin, as his later works reveal).

However, while Joyce puts most of the onus of responsibility for what he regards as a moral inertia squarely on the shoulders of the Church and the citizens themselves, he also hints at the responsibility of the British, the imperial power in Ireland, which had striven for centuries to subdue the population and obliterate all trace of Irish language and culture from the country. Molly Ivors, in 'The Dead', brings the subject to the fore in calling Gabriel a 'West Briton', and it also surfaces in 'Ivy Day' (in the controversy surrounding King Edward's visit) as well as in 'After the Race' and 'Two Gallants' where a naïve and exploited Ireland is represented by the figures of Jimmy Doyle and the forlorn harp [p. 48] respectively.

In 'Ivy Day in the Committee Room' the proposed visit to Ireland by King Edward VII provides a sounding board by which to question the principles of the two chief political candidates in the story: Richard Tierney of the rightish Nationalist party, and Colgan of the left. The question posed is whether either of them would be prepared to welcome the king to the city, the implication being that such a welcome would signal Irish acquiescence to British rule. There is a suspicion that 'Tricky Dicky' Tierney might do so:

> – But look here, John, said Mr O'Connor. Why should we welcome the king of England? Didn't Parnell himself . . .
> – Parnell, said Mr Henchy, is dead. Now here's the way I look at it. Here's this chap come to the throne after his old mother keeping him out of it till the man was grey. He's a man of the world, and he means well by us. He's a jolly fine

decent fellow, if you ask me, and no damn nonsense about him. He just says to himself: *the old one never went to see these wild Irish. By Christ, I'll go myself and see what they're like.* And are we going to insult the man when he comes over here on a friendly visit? Eh? Isn't that right, Crofton?

[p. 129]

Although 'Ivy Day' has a thorny and involved political background, Joyce does not directly take sides in this issue and the main thrust of the story is against contemporary politicians rather than their ideologies. The central political focus is on Mr Tierney, portrayed by the perfidious Mr Henchy as a scheming and unreliable opportunist whose true motive in seeking election is to achieve 'some job or other' [p. 118]. Joe Hynes regards Mr Tierney as a hypocrite and a representative of narrow middle-class interests. Others are convinced he is going to renege on payments owed to them for canvassing. These are the many versions of him. What we actually see is a nationalist movement motivated chiefly by the desire for money and drink, an assembly of timorous hypocrites, riven by jealousy and suspicion, quick to declare treachery and to spread rumour and gossip as soon as their fellow's back is turned. It is a comedy of political frailties in which the supporter of an arch-rival (Mr Crofton) is prepared to switch allegiance, to Mr Tierney. An unmistakable air of moral ignominy cleaves to the gloom of the committee room.

Mr Tierney is, of course, absent from the whole story – a point which encourages speculation and uncertainty – and yet the strength of feeling generated by his reputation creates a formidable and palpable off-stage presence. In fact all three of the key players are off-stage: Tierney, King Edward and, crucially, Parnell. All three loom as father figures over the inertness of the committee room, but only Parnell's name exudes such an aura of mythic force.

Why Parnell? Some clues to his symbolic importance and function in the story are given in the above extract, but Joyce's full effect relies on our bringing some background information to the story. Charles Stuart Parnell had been the leader and driving force of the Irish National Land League, which united Irish people of all religions and backgrounds, and he was the chief hope for bringing about Home Rule for Ireland, a hope that all but ended with his downfall in 1890 as a result of an affair with Kitty O'Shea. He was fiercely castigated by the Catholic bishops and as a consequence the scandal divided his former supporters. His political fate was eventually determined in Committee Room number 15 at the Houses of Parliament where he was voted out of office by party members, and the reference in the title of the story clearly draws an oblique parallel between the 'betrayal' of Parnell and the treatment of Mr Tierney by his agents (after Parnell's death in the following year his memory was upheld by the wearing of an ivy leaf on his anniversary; as Joe Hynes does, on p. 119). For Joyce himself, the treatment of Parnell made an early and vivid impact on him and he appears throughout his work, depicted usually as either a messianic figure or the archetypal victim of betrayal.

In 'Ivy Day' Mr O'Connor's interrupted question, 'Didn't Parnell himself . . . ?' hints that Parnell's principles would have been outraged by welcoming the king to Ireland (he had, in fact, refused to welcome Edward in 1885). Mr Henchy reminds them that, at the time of the story, Parnell is dead and he attempts to deny the symbolic force of his reputation (which Mr Hynes seeks to assert). On the other hand, as we have witnessed before, in *Dubliners* the dead often exercise a more substantial potency than the living and this is made explicit at the climax to the story by Hynes's sentimental eulogy to Parnell.

'Ivy Day in the Committee Room' is one of a group of three stories (with 'A Mother' and 'Grace') dealing with mature public life in Dublin where lame and cliched gestures are mistaken for genuine motives. They are characterised by a want of true feeling or principle in their central characters who have lost their way in terms of living meaningful lives out of a spirit of deep conviction of community. Mr Henchy, Mrs Kearney and Tom Kernan offer dim prospects for the younger figures in the early part of *Dubliners* and their already-benighted lives, and ultimately the cultural life ('A Mother') as well as the religious ('Grace') are shown to be as bankrupt as the political life in 'Ivy Day'.

What should be clear from the above discussion is how, by looking at a series of passages, you can begin to shape a sound analysis of Joyce's work. Indeed, if you look back, you will see how, just by looking at a few details from the text, it is possible to construct a complex argument about the way Joyce's text operates and how he uses language to bring his themes to life. The point about taking a series of passages is that it means you can build on your own reading of the text rather than having to accept other people's views, but also you can quickly gain confidence in seeing how to assemble an argument about the larger meaning of the text. In essence you are assembling the basic building-blocks of an essay: taking one extract, analysing it, and then moving on to develop your case further.

Essay writing is something I will take up again in the final chapter of this book, where it will become clear that the method for constructing a good essay very much follows the pattern of analysis I am using throughout the rest of the book. Of course, the method itself will not do the thinking for you, but it will help you adopt a systematic, critical approach to Joyce. For the most part the method, divided into steps, is self-evident, but in the following chapter I will be saying a little more about it as well as showing you how to apply it to Joyce's novels. Joyce can be a complex and demanding writer, but having a well-formulated, logical method will help you get the most out of his texts.

3

A *Portrait of the Artist as a Young Man*: 'an order in every way appropriate'

I Constructing an overall analysis

A PORTRAIT of the Artist as a Young Man was a radical departure for Joyce. Although Dublin is again the principal setting and some of the concerns of *Dubliners* reappear here, the strategies and style of *A Portrait* are fundamentally different – and not simply because *A Portrait* is a novel as opposed to *Dubliners* as a collection of short stories. *A Portrait* is a masterly work on its own account, but it is also an important landmark both in terms of Joyce's own development as a writer and the direction of the twentieth-century novel as a whole. Our analysis will consider all three aspects.

As a result of Joyce's innovations some readers who come to *A Portrait* expecting to read a conventional novel find it difficult at first to follow what is happening. Joyce's later writings make very few concessions to the reader and this is sometimes the case with *A Portrait*. The best advice is: persevere. If you do find some initial difficulty, try to read openly – by this I mean that on a first and second reading try to suspend any of the normal expectations of fiction and be receptive of the text's sudden shifts and feints, its linguistic plays – and the pattern of the novel will emerge more clearly.

In broad terms the novel is a study of the development of a young life, of an artist possibly, of aspects of Joyce himself certainly, but it is more than this, and a great deal of the interest of the novel springs from the very points which can be the source of difficulty, namely its formal and linguistic experiments. Keep in mind that the central figure of the novel, Stephen Dedalus, turns for his inspiration to the mythical Daedalus who is remembered for building a maze as well as for the famous waxen wings. To some extent your task is to negotiate a Joycean maze. But, at the same time, it is important to enjoy the maze for its own sake: the novel is as much about its language and its moments of consciousness, or epiphanies, as about its overall patterning.

However, in order to help get an overview of the text, it may be helpful to get some idea of the shape of surface events (all references are to the Penguin [1992] edition).

(1) After reading the novel, think about the story and what kind of pattern you can see in the text

After the opening pages of the novel, with their confused fragments of memory and childhood impressions, the focus quickly sharpens as we look through the consciousness of a very young Stephen Dedalus, son of a prosperous family living near Dublin. He is at public school, the fashionable Catholic Clongowes Wood College, where, isolated by his shyness and youth, he is at first intimidated by its ghosts and its bullies. He is preoccupied with sense impressions and language and the relationship between the two, and after suffering a feverous vision of his own death (in which these two strands meet and merge) he returns home to Dublin for Christmas. However, any relief from tension is temporary because here, amid an acrimonious quarrel at the Christmas dinner, the virulent collision of religion and politics is vividly portrayed in the clash between Stephen's father and his aunt, Dante Riordan. We next see Stephen back at school and witness the third major crisis of his early youth, as he is unjustly beaten by one of the priests. In a triumphant climax to the opening chapter Stephen redresses the injustice by way of an interview with the college rector and he emerges at the end uncomfortably victorious to the cheers of his fellow pupils.

The narrative then breaks up into a series of short fragmentary episodes that deal obliquely with the decline of Mr Dedalus's fortune. After the family moves to the Dublin suburb of Blackrock, the emphasis shifts to a mixture of adventures with friends and Stephen's own private inner world. As the imagination takes a firmer grip on his life and outlook, Stephen grows increasingly alone, often savouring his solitude, and his youth is marked by the absence of any enduring companionship. At a party, an awkward encounter with a girl ('E.C.') later moves him to write poetry in an abstracted and romanticised version of the event.

The family move to Dublin itself and here Stephen attends the less fashionable Belvedere College, again under the Jesuits, and we see his fortunes begin to take an opposite turn to those of his father. He becomes a prefect and wins a substantial prize for essay writing. Nevertheless a spirit of unrest stirs beneath the surface of these events, driving Stephen to wander through the gloomy labyrinth of Dublin's red-light district until, eventually, he swoons in the arms of a prostitute. He continues to visit the brothels until at last his torpid and lecherous existence is suddenly arrested by the reappearance at school of Father Arnall, his old Latin master from Clongowes Wood College. His menacing sermons with their vivid medieval vision of Hell's torments terrify Stephen back to the sway of the Church, and to communion with his fellow pupils.

He fervently amends his life, indulging in a monkish regime of intensive self-discipline which reaches absurd extremes. At length, however, Stephen discovers the emptiness of his penitence and his fervour subsides. This moment, in chapter 4, represents another watershed for Stephen, a leap of maturity, which enables him to reflect calmly on the future direction of his life. This new-found objectivity about his life is epitomised in an interview with the director of Belvedere, marked by heavily ironic overtones, while his rejection of the priesthood signals, too, a rejection of the Catholic Church itself. It is a crucial moment in the novel both in itself as a turning point but also in preparing for the moment when Stephen escapes to the river estuary in a rapturous affirmation of freedom and destiny. The novel reaches its emotional climax at the end of chapter 4 when Stephen, catching sight of a distant girl bathing at the water's edge, beholds her as both the revelation of his artistic destiny, and as a symbol of beauty itself, the ultimate end of art.

The spirituality of this moment contrasts starkly with the opening to chapter 5 and a vivid insight into Stephen's squalid home life with its poverty and chaos. Yet Stephen himself regards this starkness as the solid basis of his newly realised autonomy. This is demonstrated in the final chapter by episodes from university life where we see Stephen's intellectual strengths displayed in his formidable art theory as well as in his wranglings with fellow students. At the same time he is dogged by frustrated feelings about the mysterious E.C. (Emma), who has reappeared as a fellow student and who once more inspires him to compose verse, 'ten years' after his earlier effort. And yet, while these episodes reveal his undoubted intellectual resources and artistic aspirations, they reveal, too, an increasingly lonely figure, as Stephen is driven on by an uncompromising vision of freedom, a vision whose stress is fixed firmly on disengagement and rejection. He rejects any involvement with Church or politics, and towards the end we observe his increasing efforts to loosen the bonds of family and friends, until in the final pages of the novel he prepares to take flight from Ireland. The novel closes with Stephen on the brink of departure and with an invocation to his spiritual father, the mythical birdman of his namesake.

Although this summary gives a fair outline of the principal events in *A Portrait*, the novel is, of course, much more than a simple biography of a young man. As we read it we cannot help but appreciate the subtlety of its writing, the range of its feeling and experience, as well as the challenge it poses to us. Even the word 'read' takes on a new connotation with Joyce because of the unexpected demands he places on the reader. If it seems a difficult book – and most readers find it so – then you should ask yourself why and try to pinpoint the sources of this difficulty since, in doing so, you will more than likely be highlighting the key features of the novel; they will eventually appear less as problems than as portals of discovery. One reason for my saying this is that, as you will have noticed from even a cursory reading, the novel continually draws attention to itself through its different viewpoints, its extremely succinct language, its breaks and gaps in the flow – all of which seek to control the reader's attempts to make meaning of it. At the same time it is a novel which seems to evade or postpone meaning, in the process setting up oppositions and tensions in the text.

We can see that the novel is a kind of biography of Stephen Dedalus from his very early years to early manhood, and the title implies that it is a description of the early, formative life of an individual who becomes an artist. One of the important historical notes about the novel is that, unlike earlier fictive biographies, Joyce's ideas about the growth of an individual parallel those of the psychologist Sigmund Freud whose theories were gaining recognition at about the time of the novel's publication (though Joyce claimed that he did not read Freud until much later, and was always sceptical about his conclusions). The chief thrust of

Freud's theories is that the early years of a child have a profound effect on the personality of the later adult. This will not seem very revolutionary to us today, but Joyce's writing was something new in the degree to which he penetrates and reveals the workings of Stephen Dedalus's mind. His responses to situations and to people are given minute treatment and this is one reason why the surface plot or narrative in this novel is not as important as how Stephen responds to them. In a very true sense, then, a biography is not simply the outward events of a person's life but, more importantly, their influence on him/her and the process of the individual's dealing with them. In short, Joyce is concerned with the inner form of his main character, that which emerges from within.

Because of Joyce's narrative method, we understand more closely the tensions which arise in Stephen, for instance as he makes decisions or is challenged by other people or simply when he observes events (for example, an enormous energy is generated from the conflict between Stephen's pride of will and the claims and expectations made on him by his family and the Catholic Church). Much of the novel's vitality derives from these internal tensions. But there are others, some of which are thematic; for example, the conflict of religion and politics in Irish life is important and it is one that helps shape Stephen in youth and ultimately drives him from his homeland.

Not the least of these tensions is that between the reader and the text. As you will have no doubt observed in *Dubliners*, Joyce makes great demands on the reader through the narrative style of the novel, and at the root of this is Joyce's deliberate use of silence, a feature already noted at work in the earlier book. In *A Portrait* Joyce takes this a stage or two further by reducing even more the involvement of the narrator's discourse. In other words, because Stephen is telling the story and because Stephen knows where he is, the narrator often omits the usual context-setting and bridging material, and instead we have to go looking for clues as to where a scene takes place and its relationship to previous events. So where in a conventional biography we would be continually reminded of the character's age or the date, in *A Portrait* Stephen's age is only once referred to when a priest asks him during confession [see p. 156]. It is not until page 12 that we know the novel is set in Ireland, and again we discover this naturally, and obliquely, by seeing the flyleaf of a geography book. There are many such omissions – gaps and silences – in the novel, but Joyce generally supplies the clues to answering the questions he himself raises. And because Joyce so radically changes the way of writing, he also changes the reader, creates a new type of reader, one who is active in the process of the novel's meanings.

Finally, to return to the title of the novel, we must give some time in our discussion to a consideration of the idea of the 'artist'. Clearly, the title plays a crucial part in determining our expectations of the novel and of Stephen Dedalus. If the title had been *A Portrait of a Politician* or *A Portrait of a Playboy as a Young Man* we would have been led to expect different features or to judge Stephen in a different way. So Joyce's title helps to frame the novel; in a special way the title plays a key part in the novel in the manner that we read it and acts as a sort of comment from outside, especially as we have just noted Joyce's silence inside the novel. And the motto, too, 'Et ignotas animum dimittit in artes' ('And he turned his mind to explore unknown arts'), from Ovid's account of the Daedalus/Icarus myth, helps to set up a further pointer to how we are to regard Stephen, by linking him initially with Daedalus, the fabled artist-inventor, but also with Icarus, the ambitious overreacher whose blind pride and stubborn arrogance led to disaster.

I hope these ideas have helped to set the novel's 'difficulties' in perspective but, more importantly, have aroused your interest in its many facets and perhaps that you can see how they are in effect the root of the novel's enduring appeal. With such ideas buzzing about our minds we can move on to our next task, namely a start on exploring in detail the text itself. I have chosen passages from each of the five chapters of the novel and, as before, I am going to analyse them, not with any preconceived ideas about their importance, but to see what they reveal.

(2) Select a short passage from early in the novel and try to build upon the ideas you have established so far

I have decided to look at a passage from early in chapter 1, covering some of the first period in which we see Stephen Dedalus at Clongowes Wood College. It focuses on Stephen's mind and his relationship to the other boys at the school. After being shoved in a ditch and enduring a game of rugby on a cold, miserable field, he gets the first intimations of illness.

Then the higher line fellows began to come down along the matting in the middle of the refectory, Paddy Rath and Jimmy Magee and the Spaniard who was allowed to smoke cigars and the little Portuguese who wore the woolly cap. And then the lower line tables and the tables of the third line. And every single fellow had a different way of walking.

He sat in a corner of the playroom pretending to watch a game of dominos and once or twice he was able to hear for an instant the little song of the gas. The prefect was at the door with some boys and Simon Moonan was knotting his false sleeves. He was telling them something about Tullabeg.

Then he went away from the door and Wells came over to Stephen and said:

– Tell us, Dedalus, do you kiss your mother before you go to bed?

Stephen answered:

– I do.

Wells turned to the other fellows and said:

– O, I say, here's a fellow says he kisses his mother every night before he goes to bed.

The other fellows stopped their game and turned around, laughing. Stephen blushed under their eyes and said.

– I do not.

Wells said:

– O, I say, here's a fellow says he doesn't kiss his mother before he goes to bed.

They all laughed again. Stephen tried to laugh with them. He felt his whole body hot and confused in a moment. What was the right answer to the question? He had given two and still Wells laughed. But Wells must know the right answer for he was in third of grammar. He tried to think of Wells's mother but he did not dare to raise his eyes to Wells's face. He did not like Wells's face. It was Wells who had shouldered him into the square ditch the day before because he would not swop his little snuffbox for Wells's seasoned hacking chestnut, the conqueror of forty. It was a mean thing to do; all the fellows said it was. And how cold and slimy the water had been! And a fellow had once seen a big rat jump plop into the scum.

The cold slime of the ditch covered his whole body; and, when the bell rang for study and the lines filed out of the playrooms, he felt the cold air of the corridor and staircase inside his clothes. He still tried to think what was the right answer. Was it right to kiss his mother or wrong to kiss his mother? What did that mean, to kiss? You put your face up like to say goodnight and then his mother put her face down. That was to kiss. His mother put her lips on his cheek; her lips were soft and they wetted his cheek; and they made a tiny little noise: kiss. Why do people do that with their two faces?

[pp. 10–12]

I mentioned in the previous chapter that it is easier to get a fuller understanding of a passage such as this if we adopt a systematic method in which we build up an interpretation in stages. In looking at *Dubliners* my priority was to introduce Joyce in general terms and so, although I adopted a systematic approach, I decided not to make my exact method explicit. In this chapter on *A Portrait* we can concentrate more on the method which you can adopt to carry out a structured analysis of a passage. Here is the sequence we will use:

(a) *Make a short statement of what the passage is about.*
(b) *Search for an opposition or tension within the passage.*
(c) *Analyse the details of the passage, relating them to the opposition already noted.*
(d) *Try to say how the passage relates to the novel as a whole.*
(e) *Search for anything distinctive about the passage, particularly in the area of style, which you have not already noted.*

Following a sequence of steps such as this will enable you to break down the job of analysis into a series of smaller but related tasks. It also has the advantage of encouraging you to concentrate on the details of a passage which, especially with respect to a writer such as Joyce, is crucial to building up a sound understanding of a work. It will also help you to appreciate the fine nuances of meaning which Joyce is capable of achieving. Let us begin then by applying the above method to the first passage from *A Portrait.*

(a) Make a short statement of what the passage is about

Stephen is beginning to feel somewhat feverish after Wells had shoved him into the 'square ditch', or cesspool. The passage focuses on a potential nightmare of school life, bullying, and it centres on Wells's thwarted attempt to exchange Stephen's little snuffbox for his own mighty conker. The objects themselves – little snuffbox versus seasoned hacking chestnut – serve to symbolise the contrast between the small, vulnerable Stephen and the aggressive older boy. It is one of a series of passages in the early part of the chapter which vividly convey Stephen's homesickness and general discomfort at Clongowes Wood College.

(b) Search for an opposition or tension within the passage

Clearly most of the tension of the passage is generated by Wells's confrontation and Stephen's humiliation. Wells exposes Stephen's naïvety as well as his frailty, but the laughter of the older boys also reveals that Stephen is a loner, without affiliations, and this is typical of Stephen's position throughout the novel. However, Stephen's reaction to the humiliation here is not anger or resentment, as we might have expected, but confusion and then diversion. The passage reveals the thought processes of Stephen's mind and this initiates another form of tension, this time internal tension as an implicit contrast is set up between home and school, in the cosy memory of his mother's kiss amid the cold, harsh images of school. This actually has the effect of dissipating the earlier intimidation of Wells and ultimately Stephen appears to nullify its force completely by deflecting his attention onto the curious sound of the word 'kiss'.

(c) Analyse the details of the passage, relating them to the opposition already noted

After his evening meal Stephen avoids direct contact with the other boys in the playroom, choosing instead to pretend to watch a game of dominoes. The word 'pretending' in the second paragraph is an important word, for two reasons. Firstly, it indicates Stephen's attempt at cunning but also, and more importantly, Stephen is clearly trying to avoid a meeting with his tormentor, Wells, by feigning to be involved with the other boys. The presence of the prefect at the door also affords him some protection, and his departure is Wells's cue to approach and bait him again. In spite of the square ditch incident Stephen is not at first cowed by his antagonist; his replies are assertive, but then later he becomes confused. His confusion is revealed, of course, by his perplexity after the fellows' laughter, but notice how the tension of the initial confrontation is sustained in the second half of the extract where it moves inside Stephen's mind. His frustration is portrayed by the confusion of his thoughts, set out in short, abrupt statements, his earlier assertiveness now turned inward in the form of silent, but fevered indignation.

The passage also stresses how much Stephen is a loner. He is younger than the other boys and does not take an active part in their games. The ease with which Wells torments him suggests that Stephen has not yet made any strong alliances, as Wells himself obviously has, and so he cannot escape from this harassment. Wells's teasing questions have the undoubted effect of intensifying his detachment since his contradictory answers clearly make him the butt of the other boys' humour – particularly as his second reply is a disastrous attempt to restore his self-esteem. His replies reveal how he would like to be accepted by them, in that they seek to conform to the expectations implicit in the questions, and yet he seems to be intrinsically separate by disposition as well as by age. Moreover, his references to the fellows reveal his slight awe of them and his ignorance of the right answer increases the gap still more, at the same time increasing Stephen's confusion since he is convinced that Wells must already know the correct reply. Morally he both respects Wells as an authority figure and despises him for his unmanly conduct over the snuffbox. It is, as such, a small but important step in the demystification and diminishment of authority – as the rest of chapter 1, and chapter 2 will show.

(d) Try to say how the passage relates to the novel as a whole
In the first place, we can see clearly how the passage reveals the way in which Stephen's thoughts of home promise a refuge from the unpleasant realities of school. Most of the opening chapter's events expose or emphasise Stephen's discomfort, usually in the form of conflicts, both at school and at home (for example, the fierce clash between Mrs Riordan and his father at the Christmas dinner). His painful school experiences heighten feelings of home-sickness which he has endured since his mother and father left him at the college with instructions never to speak with the 'rough boys' and never to 'peach on a fellow' [pp. 5, 6]. He is continually reminded of them and their instructions are tested frequently, as in the above passage where Stephen upholds his father's code by not peaching on one of the 'rough boys', over the square ditch episode, in spite of the fact that everyone agrees it was a mean thing of Wells to do. The interrogation about his mother strikes at his homesickness, while his cosy, idealised images of home make a stark contrast with the stress and confusion of the strange school, and at the same time focuses our attention on the theme of famil-ial relationships which will later become a central issue in the novel.

These recollections of home by Stephen are typical of the pro-cess by which his consciousness is continually expanding to embrace contexts outside of his immediate situation, a process which deepens and enriches the reader's experience of the novel. Another characteristic feature of Stephen's mental processes at this stage is his habit of differentiating between sense impressions, for example by setting cold/slimy images against warm/cosy ones, and this can be considered as an early suggestion of his artis-tic sensitivity. Akin to this is the fact that he is also an acute, detached, observer of the fine details and events around him, and spends much of his time shaping his observations into order. In fact the need for order is a prominent aspect of his outlook both here and later. In the above extract he observes with childlike astonishment how 'every single fellow had a different way of walking'. He has earlier noted that all the boys have different fathers and mothers, and different clothes and voices, and while one of the overt purposes of the opening chapters is to reveal Stephen's strong academic potential, it also tells us a great deal about his sensitive interaction with the world around him, absorbing impressions of it and shaping his own reality from it.

(e) Search for anything distinctive about the passage, particularly in the area of style, which you have not already noted

One difficulty created for the reader at this stage in the novel arises from the fact that the young Stephen himself appears to be narrating the story from his own immature point of view. The narrative uses his language and, as we would expect perhaps, the diction and syntax reflect this immaturity, with simple vocabulary and simple, direct sentences that are often short but frequently linked with the ubiquitous conjunction 'and'. Stephen acts not only as the arranger of the material but as the commentator on it too, while Joyce remains behind or outside of it. And although Stephen is a thoughtful, inward individual he naturally cannot make mature judgements on himself, so it is let to the reader to do this. As you may have already noticed, it is an approach that does not make concessions to the reader and it is an increasingly typical feature of Joyce's style. Further, because Stephen is the arranger we get a raw-looking series of fragments which at first reading can appear as a jumbled mess, devoid as it is of the usual bridging discourse from the narrator to guide us round the fragments. We get the apparently half-digested experiences as structured by Stephen's mind in the order in which it recalls them, a series of flashbacks placed immediately before us, but expressed in the idiom of his youth.

The absence of the narrator's discourse also means that there is no commentary either to explain the relationships between passages or to tell us why they have been selected; in other words we are not told what the importance of these passages is, and they sometimes appear at first isolated and enigmatic in these terms. The answer is that they are all important, since they are all selected and arranged by their character-narrator, but it is left to the reader to explore and establish their importance. In fact such passages or epiphanies are not isolated or unconnected but are part of a pattern of archetypes from which we establish meaning (the above passage outlines a typical crisis for Stephen and reveals the method by which he copes with it, a method he employs more and more as the novel progresses). However, the 'silent' Joyce himself only makes meanings available, without making them explicit or favouring a particular interpretation. In this way we, the readers, should be prepared to take an active part in the process of creating meaning.

(3) Select a second passage for discussion

The following passage is taken from near the beginning of chapter 2.

He was sitting in the midst of a children's party at Harold's Cross. His silent watchful manner had grown upon him and he took little part in the games. The children, wearing the spoils of their crackers, danced and romped noisily and, though he tried to share their merriment, he felt himself a gloomy figure amid the gay cocked hats and sunbonnets.

But when he had sung his song and withdrawn into a snug corner of the room he began to taste the joy of his loneliness. The mirth, which in the beginning of the evening had seemed to him false and trivial, was like a soothing air to him, passing gaily by his senses, hiding from other eyes the feverish agitation of his blood while through the circling of the dancers and amid the music and laughter her glance travelled to his corner, flattering, taunting, searching, exciting his heart.

In the hall the children who had stayed latest were putting on their things: the party was over. She had thrown a shawl about her and, as they went together towards the tram, sprays of her fresh warm breath flew gaily about her cowled head and her shoes tapped blithely on the glassy road.

It was the last tram. The lank brown horses knew it and shook their bells to the clear night in admonition. The conductor talked with the driver, both nodding often in the green light of the lamp. On the empty seats of the tram were scattered a few coloured tickets. No sound of footsteps came up or down the road. No sound broke the peace of the night save when the lank brown horses rubbed their noses together and shook their bells.

They seemed to listen, he on the upper and she on the lower. She came up to his step many times and went down to hers again between their phrases and once or twice stood close beside him for some moments on the upper step, forgetting to go down, and then went down. His heart danced upon her movements like a cork upon a tide. He heard what her eyes said to him from beneath their cowl and knew that in some dim past, whether in life or in revery, he had heard their tale before. He saw her urge her vanities, her fine dress and sash and long black stockings, and knew that he had yielded to them a thousand times. Yet a voice within him spoke above the noise of his dancing heart, asking him would he take her gift to which he had only to stretch out his hand. And he remembered the day when he and Eileen had stood looking into the hotel grounds, watching the waiters running up a trail of bunting on the flagstaff and the fox terrier scampering to and fro on the sunny lawn, and how, all of a sudden, she had broken out into a peal of laughter and had run down the sloping curve of the path. Now, as then, he stood listlessly in his place, seeming a tranquil watcher of the scene before him.

– She too wants me to catch hold of her, he thought. That's why she came with me to the tram. I could easily catch hold of her when she comes up to my step: nobody is looking. I could hold her and kiss her.

But he did neither: and, when he was sitting alone in the deserted tram, he tore his ticket into shreds and stared gloomily at the corrugated footboard.

[pp. 71–3]

(a) Make a short statement of what the passage is about
The Dedalus family have moved from the comfortable home of chapter 1, first to an outer suburb to the south of Dublin (Blackrock), and then a 'flight' to Dublin city itself, 'a new and complex sensation' for Stephen. To illustrate the complexities of Stephen's new life, Joyce presents three very short episodes concerning encounters with girls (each beginning with the words 'He was sitting . . . ' [pp. 70–2]). The above passage is the third of these. It describes a party and its epilogue, a set of events which impinge very vividly on Stephen's consciousness such that immediately after it he is inspired to write what appear to be his first verses. Where the two preceding episodes hint obscurely at incipient sexuality, the third, above, deals with this theme more directly and anticipates one of the second chapter's principal concerns. It expresses clearly Stephen's inability to connect, first with other party-goers and then with E.C., and reveals the obstacles within himself. It also hints at murmuring internal conflicts within him which become more clearly formulated later in the novel.

(b) Search for an opposition or tension within the passage
The tensions in the passage are internal, originating in oppositions within Stephen himself. As in the previous passage, Stephen is alone even though he is now among other party-goers. And again he is a detached observer. While the reader may be aware of some tension here, Stephen himself does not appear to be because, although at first he tries to engage with the party, he eventually comes to 'taste the joy of his loneliness'. Not only has he not come to terms with the solitude that he invariably finds himself in, but he actively avoids the group of other children, finding the merriment 'false and trivial'. While he takes no part in the merrymaking it agitates him and he eventually finds it exciting, at

least distantly. In the same way, the second part of the passage, at the tram stop, reveals, through its details and tensions, more about Stephen than about the materialistic details of the scene or of the girl he escorts to it. One thing that is clear is Stephen's response to the moment. Where in the first part we are told that Stephen savours his solitude at the party, later we directly observe his feelings of frustration at the his inability to reach out and kiss the girl, whom we later know as E.C. ('Emma').

(c) Analyse the details of the passage, relating them to the opposition already noted
As Stephen watches the girl step up and down from the tram, notice how Joyce matches inner and outer states. At the party the 'feverish agitation of his blood' is matched by the circling movement of the dancers amid music and laughter. Stephen gives a contrasting outward show of control or quiet, and then, at the tram stop, an outwardly calm scene of quiet in which the tram men talk imperceptibly, the cold night is the prelude to the storm of Stephen's feelings. Equally, at the tram stop the unrest in his 'dancing heart' reflects the tantalising movement of the girl on the steps ('His heart danced upon her movements like a cork'). The turmoil is, of course, intensified by his failure to act and even more by his awareness of this failure.

(d) Try to say how the passage relates to the novel as a whole
Joyce hints that the root of Stephen's frustration, his failure to act, lies in his emotional detachment: he lives too far apart from the scenes in which he 'takes part'. Here, as the moment approaches a climax, Stephen is described as a 'tranquil watcher of the scene before him', and we know that he will not bring the moment to a satisfactory climax because he cannot engage with it; the crisis in his blood is too much under control as his tendency to verbalise the situation makes clear. The crisis is reflected in the words concerning movement and activity; for instance, consider the words used to describe the effect of 'E.C' on Stephen when their eyes meet during the party – flattering, taunting, searching, exciting. In effect they refer to Stephen's sexual arousal and this awakening sexuality is another, more important, reason for his separateness from the other children at the party. Furthermore, that they both meet at the end of the party and walk toward the last tram highlights their attraction for each other, while the fact that it is the last

tram emphasises how Stephen puts off making any move to the last possible moment.

The passage appears amid a number of references to sexuality and sexual uncertainty. In a chapter that brilliantly evokes the anxieties and uncertainties of adolescence, Stephen's stirring, incipient sexuality is at first uncertain too. In the passage immediately before the above extract he is mistaken for a girl called Josephine and then later another boy (Bertie Tallon) is mistaken for a girl during the college play. So, in a different way, the encounter with E.C. is a test of sexuality for Stephen. I think it is for this reason that towards the end of our extract above, as the moment approaches its climax, the narrator suddenly inserts a memory of Stephen with another girl, Eileen, at a hotel. On the face of it, this enigmatic episode in the hotel grounds seems unrelated to what is happening here. But the point which unites the two moments is the fact that in both encounters Stephen is a passive spectator to the two girls. What it was that Eileen laughed at is not clear, but we can make a reasonable guess if we recall the previous occasion in chapter 1 when Stephen described the day with Eileen at the hotel. It is described on page 43 in words almost identical to those here. Stephen now recalls the hotel and the fox terrier, but the bit he omits is important because it points up his embarrassment now. Eileen had placed her hand in his pockets and, of course, felt his penis but, being very young, he had remarked only on how cool, soft and thin her hands were, while she had run away laughing at what she had discovered there. Eileen's mocking laughter ridicules him now and points up his ineffectualness, while his omission of the key sentence reveals his awareness of this in the context of his newly awoken sexual feelings. His later response to his failure, alone in the deserted tram, is to tear his ticket into shreds in a mood which recalls the anticlimax of 'Araby' when the boy, not unlike Stephen, is moved by a similar stirring of sexuality towards Mangan's sister.

Eileen is never mentioned again after this episode and E.C. ('Emma') now takes over as a distant, idealised object of sexual fantasy. Frustration over his failure with E.C. at the tram stop eventually drives Stephen to explore the red-light district of Dublin in search of sexual fulfilment, and he achieves a sort of success at the end of the chapter when he swoons in the sensuous embrace of a prostitute – though even there he is still represented as the passive participant.

(e) Search for anything distinctive about the passage, particularly in the area of style, which you have not already noted

One of the unusual features of this novel that you may have noticed already is the strict control of the narrator's point of view of events in it, and in particular how rigidly the narrator limits the point of view in the novel to that of Stephen himself. We see things only through Stephen's eyes. For instance, the party does not include anyone's feelings other than Stephen's and the attitude to his isolation from the others is Stephen's own, not the narrator's – the narrator does not see Stephen through the eyes of any of the other children at the party. Similarly on the tram, only Stephen's point of view is given: he sees the (unnamed) girl and notes only her physical appearance, 'her vanities', which really tell us more about Stephen's state of mind than about her. In fact the girl is very shadowy altogether and we learn even less of her than Stephen does; she is unnamed here and we only know her later enigmatically as E.C. The selection of material is Stephen's and it is very selective; when he later composes his verse about the scene [p. 73] he is even more selective in idealising the moment, mentioning neither the tram nor the horses and with only a shadowy presentation of the two protagonists. As a result of this strict control we receive a consistent viewpoint whose perceptions reveal Stephen's personality as well as his states of mind and, in addition, we get a more or less constant monitoring of his mind, all of which helps to construct a deep and intimate psychological reality.

On the other hand, see how Joyce brilliantly evokes the tram-stop scene through its carefully observed details: 'sprays of her fresh warm breath', 'her shoes tapped blithely', the bells of the 'lank brown horses', the simple movement of the tram men all picked out in the green light of the tram. In a few simple but deft touches Joyce captures simultaneously both the intensity of feeling in the young Stephen's agitated blood, and the fragile and mysterious evanescence of the moment. And Joyce succeeds while still employing an idiom in agreement with Stephen's own level of language with simple diction and syntax, using Stephen's consciousness for the point of view and responses to it.

(4) Select a third passage for discussion

The third passage is taken from chapter 3.

Every word of it was for him. Against his sin, foul and secret, the whole wrath of God was aimed. The preacher's knife had probed deeply into his diseased conscience and he felt now that his soul was festering in sin. Yes, the preacher was right. God's turn had come. Like a beast in its lair his soul had lain down in its own filth but the blasts of the angel's trumpet had driven him forth from the darkness of sin into the light. The words of doom cried by the angel shattered in an instant his presumptuous peace. The wind of the last day blew through his mind; his sins, the jeweleyed harlots of his imagination, fled before the hurricane, squeaking like mice in their terror and huddled under a mane of hair.

As he crossed the square, walking homeward, the light laughter of a girl reached his burning ear. The frail gay sound smote his heart more strongly than a trumpetblast, and, not daring to lift his eyes, he turned aside and gazed, as he walked, into the shadow of the tangled shrubs. Shame rose from his smitten heart and flooded his whole being. The image of Emma appeared before him and, under her eyes, the flood of shame rushed forth anew from his heart. If she knew to what his mind had subjected her or how his brutelike lust had torn and trampled upon her innocence! Was that boyish love? Was that chivalry? Was that poetry? The sordid details of his orgies stank under his very nostrils: the soot-coated packet of pictures which he had hidden in the flue of the fireplace and in the presence of whose shameless or bashful wantonness he lay for hours sinning in thought and deed; his monstrous dreams, peopled by apelike creatures and by harlots with gleaming jewel eyes; the foul long letters he had written in the joy of guilty confession and carried secretly for days and days only to throw them under cover of night among the grass in the corner of a field or beneath some hingeless door or in some niche in the hedges where a girl might come upon them as she walked by and read them secretly. Mad! Mad! Was it possible he had done these things? A cold sweat broke out upon his forehead as the foul memories condensed within his brain.

When the agony of shame had passed from him he tried to raise his soul from its abject powerlessness. God and the Blessed Virgin were too far from him: God was too great and stern and the Blessed Virgin too pure and holy. But he imagined that he stood near Emma in a wide land and, humbly and in tears, bent and kissed the elbow of her sleeve.

[pp. 123–5]

(a) Make a short statement of what the passage is about

This is the first chance we have of seeing Stephen's reaction to the opening shots in Father Arnall's sermon during the Belvedere College 'retreat'. These opening shots deal with death and judgement and we can see how the sermon is beginning to take its effect on Stephen, forcing him to reflect for the first time on his sins. On one level, in physical terms, Stephen's sins consist of indulging in sexual fantasy and masturbation inspired by pornographic pictures and wantonness. He has also tried to corrupt others by writing obscene letters and leaving them to be discovered by innocent girls. Although we are aware that Stephen has been visiting prostitutes, such visits do not immediately spring to his mind as sinful. On the other hand, he is acutely sensitive to his own state of guilt and this is projected onto and intensified by his image of Emma who, having once represented for him the unattainable object of his lust, is now transformed into the equally unattainable object of purity and childhood innocence. Here (in the third paragraph of our extract) she acts as a foil, a simple contrast to the tortuous ways of sin and desire.

(b) Search for an opposition or tension within the passage
The passage is dominated by deep internal tensions generated by Stephen's emotional response to Father Arnall's words. Clearly, the tension arises from the violent threat in the preacher's words, playing on Stephen's conscience, now isolated from other people and from the prospect of escape from shame. The opposition in the passage is a complex one but it is one that involves the conflict between Stephen's previous actions and his growing regret, at the heart of which is a deep sense of shame. This sense, and the tension too, is increased by Stephen's realisation of helplessness in the face of God's imagined wrath. Where in the past he has sinned in secret, under cover of darkness, he finds himself now driven forth 'from the darkness of sin into the light' – of God's retribution.

(c) Analyse the details of the passage, relating them to the opposition already noted
What Stephen feels deeply here is not guilt about his actions so much as shame at having been 'discovered' in them. We can see this from Stephen's reflection on his sins, about the middle of the passage. He scolds himself for having trampled on Emma's image through his 'brutelike lust' and then confronts his sins by asking 'Was that boyish love? Was that chivalry? Was that poetry?' By doing this, he himself points up the opposition between his spiritual ideals and his sordid fantasies. These ideals can be traced back to the time of his days in Blackrock at the beginning of chapter 2 when, fired by echoes from his reading, he sported with romanticised gestures of dutiful obedience and simple adventure. So the present passage looks back with nostalgia and disappointment to his prepubescent youth, a lost time of innocence. Of course, the reappearance of Father Arnall, his Latin master from Clongowes

Wood College, is also a key factor, forming a bridge between present and past states.

Stephen's reference to chivalry in the passage also sets up a contrast between his past and present perceptions of women. It undoubtedly increases his feelings of shame but it has an important ironic effect, too, because we should remember that even during the time of Stephen's sins and visits to the prostitutes he is also a prefect in the Sodality of Our Blessed Lady; he is, again like the boy of the 'Araby' story, a knight of the Virgin, and as such is expected to be a spotless example to his fellows. This point depicts Stephen as even more of a hypocrite and emphasises his fraudulent position: he is in fact one of the 'whited sepulchres' to which Father Arnall refers in his opening sermon, and it is for this reason that Stephen considers that 'Every word was for him'.

Although Stephen has always been aware of this hypocrisy and of his indifference to it, in the light of the preacher's onslaught his position is now entirely altered through shame, and this accounts for the peculiar role which Emma plays in the above passage. While she is the desecrated symbol of both innocence and experience, she is also the symbolic source of atonement because Stephen imagines he must approach her for forgiveness. This is forced on him because his shame combined with the falsehood of his position as a prefect of the Virgin prevents him from addressing the Virgin herself. Through this process, therefore, Emma comes to represent a complex fusion of three opposing symbols: unassailable virginity, a fantasised object of Stephen's lust, and a source of merciful grace.

(d) Try to say how the passage relates to the novel as a whole
One important point about this passage is that it gives us new information about how Stephen's mind works. The focus in the passage is firmly fixed on Stephen's internal states, revealing a new side to him. Far from the insouciant, idle, careless fellow of the start of the chapter, we observe a terrified Stephen who will be cowed back to the clutches of the Church by the close of chapter 3. For the time being, however, his ego still looms large, his spirit remains unbroken, even undamaged, and his pride here makes him resilient to the blows of Father Arnall's opening shots. Even in the above passage as he feels shamed we can see hints of his pride: 'Every word of it was for him' and 'Was it possible that he had done these things?'

The preacher's sermon has only just started when we get the above response. Already Stephen is stirred by his reflection on sinful deeds, and the sermons will increasingly gather momentum and emotional intensity. Until now we have seen Stephen's personal star in the ascendant, against a background of continuing decline and confusion at home. He has been left to himself, to explore unchecked the city and himself, his feelings and his bodily nature. The consequence has been lethargy at school and a sort of lassitude of spirit, but this has all been valuable experience in raw reality. Until now the Church has had a mainly implicit, impalpable part in his development. The sermons therefore mark a radical change in the course of the narrative because we see Stephen's free development checked; he will be forced back to the Church, and not by rational means but by fear and shame working on a preformed set of values rigorously ingrained by the Church itself. Thus Stephen's response is to withdraw back into those values. In a real sense, the sermons are a literal 'retreat' for Stephen, a withdrawal into outmoded ways of thinking, a medieval attitude to ethics based on unquestioning acquiescence and conformity. In this way the chapter marks an arrest of Stephen's artistic development.

(e) Search for anything distinctive about the passage, particularly in the area of style, which you have not already noted
The changes in Stephen's progress are reflected in the language too. The mode of narration remains the same: experience is still filtered through Stephen's own consciousness, but in the imagery of corruption and decay – words like 'festering', 'diseased', 'filth', 'foul', 'stank' – we can recognise an increasingly familiar focus for Stephen, on the sordid realities of experience, as well as something of the verbal flavour of his initial 'sin'. But there is in this diction, too, something of the style of Father Arnall's sermon itself, a point which indicates the depth of influence that the priest and the Church has on Stephen's mind. In addition, the grotesquerie of the imagery (whose intensity increases dramatically from this point on) further helps to heighten the tensions of the passage by helping to convey the feverishness of Stephen's tortured thoughts (for example, 'monstrous dreams', 'apelike creatures', 'jeweleyed harlots'). It reveals how during the retreat Stephen becomes more and more cut off from the realities of the everyday world, and turns inward to focus on the psychological

realities of his soul and the past. By setting up Stephen's intense feverishness in chapter 3 Joyce cleverly prepares the way for the irony in the opening pages of the next chapter and a new relationship between Stephen and the reader.

(5) Select a fourth passage for discussion

The fourth passage is taken from chapter 4.

He was passing at that moment before the jesuit house in Gardiner Street, and wondered vaguely which window would be his if he ever joined the order. Then he wondered at the vagueness of his wonder, at the remoteness of his soul from what he had hitherto imagined her sanctuary, at the frail hold which so many years of order and obedience had of him when once a definite and irrevocable act of his threatened to end for ever, in time and in eternity, his freedom. The voice of the director urging upon him the proud claims of the church and the mystery and power of the priestly office repeated itself idly in his memory. His soul was not there to hear and greet it and he knew now that the exhortation he had listened to had already fallen into an idle formal tale. He would never swing the thurible before the tabernacle as priest. His destiny was to be elusive of social or religious orders. The wisdom of the priest's appeal did not touch him to the quick. He was destined to learn his own wisdom apart from others or to learn the wisdom of others himself wandering among the snares of the world.

The snares of the world were its ways of sin. He would fall. He had not yet fallen but he would fall silently, in an instant. Not to fall was too hard, too hard: and he felt the silent lapse of his soul, as it would be at some instant to come, falling, falling but not yet fallen, still unfallen but about to fall.

He crossed the bridge over the stream of the Tolka and turned his eyes coldly for an instant towards the faded blue shrine of the Blessed Virgin which stood fowlwise on a pole in the middle of a hamshaped encampment of poor cottages. Then bending to the left, he followed the lane which led up to his house. The faint sour stink of rotted cabbages came towards him from the kitchengardens on the rising ground above the river. He smiled to think that it was this disorder, the misrule and confusion of his father's house and the stagnation of vegetable life, which was to win the day in his soul. Then a short laugh broke from his lips as he thought of that solitary farmhand in the kitchengardens behind their house whom they had nicknamed the man with the hat. A second laugh, taking rise from the first after a pause, broke from him involuntarily as he thought of how the man with the hat worked, considering in turn the four points of the sky and then regretfully plunging his spade in the earth.

He pushed open the latchless door of the porch and passed through the naked hallway into the kitchen. A group of his brothers and sisters was sitting round the table. Tea was nearly over and only the last of the second watered tea remained in the bottoms of the small glassjars and jampots which did service for teacups. Discarded crusts and lumps of sugared bread, turned brown by the tea which had been poured over them, lay scattered on the table. Little wells of tea lay here and there on the board and a knife with a broken ivory handle was stuck through the pith of a ravaged turnover.

The sad quiet greyblue glow of the dying day came through the window and the open door, covering over and allaying quietly a sudden instinct of remorse in Stephen's heart. All that had been denied them had been freely given to him, the eldest: but the quiet glow of evening showed him in their faces no sign of rancour.

He sat near them at the table and asked where his father and mother were. One answered:

– Goneboro toboro lookboro atboro aboro houseboro.

Still another removal! A boy named Fallon in Belvedere had often asked him with a silly laugh why they moved so often. A frown of scorn darkened quickly on his forehead as he heard again the silly laugh of the questioner.

[pp. 175–7]

(a) Make a short statement of what the passage is about

Having been interviewed by the director of Belvedere College concerning the possibility of a vocation to the priesthood, Stephen is at first drawn to the prospect and then, as the above passage shows, repelled by it in spite of the aura of mystery and power offered by the Jesuit office. He rejects the idea and the passage shows his satisfaction at his decision; although he has no notion yet of where his life may lead, he is exhilarated by its newly asserted freedom.

The above passage comes as Stephen returns home, and as he approaches the depressed area where he lives, with its ugliness and confusion, he happily contemplates the contrast between his home life and the ordered life of the Jesuits. The inside of his father's house is no better but Stephen finds assurance in its squalor. He is moved, briefly, by the sorry condition of his brothers – the first time that we see him and them together – and he feels a twinge of remorse that they have been denied the opportunities freely bestowed on himself. He discovers that they are to be evicted again – yet another family removal to keep ahead of the bailiff. It is another point on the curve of his father's inexorable decline.

However, the passage marks an important moment of stillness between two climaxes: his interview with the director and, at the end of the chapter, his encounter on the estuary beach with a girl whose beauty has a profound symbolic effect on Stephen's imagination and his sense of destiny.

(b) Search for an opposition or tension within the passage

Although there is an unmistakable air of stillness, even resignation, in the anticlimax after Stephen's interview with the director, there is here both a tone of restrained triumph (with echoes of the mood at the conclusion of chapter 1) and also evidence of underlying conflicts and tensions, which arise as a result of this restraint. Some of this tension results from the clash of Stephen's own pride and the 'proud claims' of the Church. We can compare Stephen's response here with that in our previous passage where he is profoundly moved by the voice of the Church and, quite apart from the shame or guilt which follows his sins, he is very much aware of the part played by pride in his defiance of the Church in chapters 2 and 3. Now, however, he transcends this conflict; his pride is less assertive because his rejection of the Church stems not from the triumph of his vanity but from the realisation that the Church has no part to play in his 'destiny'. The Church is irrelevant to his life. However, Stephen's pride carries him through and imbues him with a renewed air of self-assurance.

The contrast between the disorder of his home life and that promised by the Jesuits presents a more fundamental opposition. In addition to power and an insight into the mysteries of the faith, the Church also offers security. Furthermore, Stephen is conscious that the Jesuits are an élite order both in terms of their privileged role in the Catholic Church and in terms of their intellectual reputation. They would offer a direction for his burgeoning intellect and a sense of purpose, a mission indeed, for his drifting life. On the other hand, his home life appears to promise only 'misrule and chaos' and the continuing spiral of degradation. And yet this disorder wins the day in his soul, suggesting that its now familiar squalor offers a sort of integrity to his spirit of defiance.

(c) Analyse the details of the passage, relating them to the opposition already noted

It is not difficult to see, I hope, that again one of the key words in this passage, as in the novel as a whole, is 'order'. As a theme it appears throughout the novel in a variety of guises and forms: for instance, in the forms at Clongowes Wood, and in the religious order, the ranks within the Church and especially that of the Jesuits under whose tutelage Stephen has been almost continuously since the start, and also in the theme of decorum or correct behaviour. In metaphorical terms, the order represents a sense of place and also discipline, each of which holds a very important place in Stephen's consciousness. For Stephen the 'order' of the

Catholic Church presents here both security and a sense of identity (in simple terms, his own 'window' as a priest in the Gardiner
Street house which in the above extract he passes on his way
home). At the same time, the cost of this is, of course, the loss of
freedom, a yielding to the tyranny of the 'chill and order' and to
the regulation of a life in which his pride of will would be broken
and subsumed by the Church. It is this pride of will that has been
the driving force of Stephen, and which eventually enables him to
recognise his destiny as well as the means of reaching it. Pride also
permits Stephen increasingly to withstand the multitude of voices
around him which he interprets as a constant charge or demand
on his progress, threatening to seize and claim him for some other
cause.

Consequently, Stephen reflects that his destiny is to be 'elusive
of social or religious orders'. It is a key statement for him, register-
ing a new level of inner maturity. Yet in spite of this assertion, the
mood of this passage is anticlimactic and quiet, with even a hint of
resignation about it, and this is curious in the wake of such a landmark in his life. The reason is that his decision is essentially a
negative one, of rejection, and the climax to the chapter comes
later with the triumphant vision of the girl on the sea-shore, the
moment in which he positively embraces what he takes to be his
destiny as an artist.

However, at this moment, in the passage, Stephen is not aware
of any *particular* destiny as such and is more concerned to safe-
guard his freedom. He voices his terror of making an 'irrevocable
act' of commitment which would destroy forever his freedom, and
it is this threat which preserves his freedom now. So here, as in
chapter 2, Stephen simply regards himself as marked out for
something special but unknown and in effect uses the term 'destiny' to designate an as-yet unformulated aspiration as a pretext
for postponing a decision. We get the impression that Stephen is
more concerned to preserve his freedom for its own intrinsic sake,
thus avoiding any commitment or involvement and deferring a decision on his future.

(d) Try to say how the passage relates to the novel as a whole
The passage depicts several facets of Stephen's life: its disorder,
his turning away from the Jesuits to the confusion of home, and
the re-emergence of his provisional if negative concept of a personal destiny ('elusive of social or religious orders'). We are told

that he 'crossed the bridge', which in addition to its literal meaning carries unmistakable metaphorical force too, implying that he has taken a decisive step into the next phase of his life, or at least away from the last. He has chosen to learn the wisdom of the world through, as the narrator puts it, 'the snares of the world', a thrust which is echoed on the final page of the book when Stephen affirms his intention to meet head on with the raw life of the everyday world, the stuff of experience which, as an artist, he will hope to transmute into the permanent life of art. Here, such raw material is hinted at in the disorder of his father's house and life, its squalor and degradation and inexorable decline. He opts for the humanity of existence, with its dirt and chaos, as well as the pitiable acquiescence of his brothers and sisters.

(e) Search for anything distinctive about the passage, particularly in the area of style, which you have not already noted

If we look at the language of this passage and compare it with that in previous passages we can see again how this has modulated to reflect Stephen's development with more mature vocabulary and syntax. However, the modulation of style has now reached a crucial stage. For the first time in the novel we can say that the language of Stephen's inner reflections is on the same level as the language of the narrator's voice, whereas in previous chapters we are always aware of the gap between the immature Stephen and the dominant narrator, who nevertheless adopted Stephen's language and point of view to intensify the narrative. Now we may feel more convincingly that Stephen is the narrator of his own story. The subtle cadences are Stephen's, and the mood of resignation and stillness matches his sense of reconciliation to whatever fate holds in store.

There is a sense, too, in which Stephen dominates the language and uses it, rather than the reverse. Look again at the second paragraph in the extract above and listen to the musical effect of the narrator's repetition of the word 'fall'. The resonant play on this word mirrors perfectly the way that Stephen has previously encountered reality by turning it into poetry, and at the same time his play on the word withdraws all of its previous threat (remember how the same word in chapter 3 terrified him to the core). In other words by exploiting the poetic musicality of a word like this, he reduces its power over him. So, in the passage, by contemplating the doom of his soul he appears to be untouched by the reality

behind the thought and there is even a hint of frisson at the realisation of his own power over it.

(6) Select a fifth passage for discussion

The fifth extract comes from towards the close of the final chapter
of the novel, covering the last days of Stephen's period at university.

How could he hit their conscience or how cast his shadow over the imagination
of their daughters, before their squires begat upon them, that they might breed a
race less ignoble than their own? And under the deepened dusk he felt the
thoughts and desires of the race to which he belonged flitting like bats, across the
dark country lanes, under trees by the edges of streams and near the poolmottled
bogs. A woman had waited in the doorway as Davin had passed by at night and,
offering him a cup of milk, had all but wooed him to her bed; for Davin had the
mild eyes of one who could be secret. But him no woman's eyes had wooed.
   His arm was taken in a strong grip and Cranly's voice said:
   – Let us eke go.
   They walked southward in silence. Then Cranly said:
   – That blithering idiot Temple! I swear to Moses, do you know, that I'll be the
death of that fellow one time.
   But his voice was no longer angry and Stephen wondered was he thinking of
her greeting to him under the porch.
   They turned to the left and walked on as before. When they had gone on so for
some time Stephen said:
   – Cranly, I had an unpleasant quarrel this evening.
   – With your people? Cranly asked.
   – With my mother.
   – About religion?
   – Yes, Stephen answered.
   After a pause Cranly asked:
   – What age is your mother?
   – Not old, Stephen said. She wishes me to make my easter duty.
   – And will you?
   – I will not, Stephen said.
   – Why not? Cranly said.
   – I will not serve, answered Stephen.
   – That remark was made before, Cranly said calmly.
   – It is made now, said Stephen hotly.
   Cranly pressed Stephen's arm, saying:
   – Go easy, my dear man. You're an excitable bloody man, do you know.
   He laughed nervously as he spoke and, looking up into Stephen's face with
moved and friendly eyes, said:
   – Do you know that you are an excitable man?
   – I daresay I am, said Stephen, laughing also.
   Their minds, lately estranged, seemed suddenly to have been drawn closer, one

to the other.
   – Do you believe in the eucharist? Cranly asked.
   – I do not, Stephen said.
   – Do you disbelieve then?
   – I neither believe in it nor disbelieve in it, Stephen answered.
   – Many persons have doubts, even religious persons, yet they overcome them or put them aside, Cranly said. Are your doubts on that point too strong?
   – I do not wish to overcome them, Stephen answered.

[pp. 259–60]

(a) Make a short statement of what the passage is about
Returning from the library, Stephen and his friend Cranly walk past a plush Dublin hotel. Stephen stares into its drawing room and, reflecting on the comfortable lives of its affluent, landed patrons, muses on how as a writer he might reach their complacent and insulated minds. His thoughts flicker back to Davin's story of how once on a trip to the country a peasant woman had tried to seduce him, an adventure Stephen has had no experience of. The extract then reveals Stephen's current difficulties with his family, in particular the conflict between his mother's strict religious expectations of him and his own free-thinking, expansive mind; he sees her demands as encroaching on what he has come to regard as the essential requirement of the artist, his freedom.

(b) Search for an opposition or a tension within the passage
The tensions of the passage arise from the question of ties of family and friendship. Ostensibly, these tensions emerge from the conflict between Stephen and Cranly, but this is just a substitute for the deeper conflict between Stephen and his mother in terms of religion, and of his general relationship with his family, his ties with which have become increasingly weaker since the start of the chapter. As a result his mother has resisted Stephen's struggle to free himself of what he has come to regard as obstacles on the road to freedom of mind. Her resistance can be traced back to chapter 4 where we are told that she had been 'hostile to the idea' of university, and it is now increasing towards its eventual climax in the demand that Stephen make his Easter duty – in other words, that he receive Holy Communion during this period, the minimum duty for a Roman Catholic. This would also necessitate his making a full confession and submitting himself to the will of the Church and effectively it would mean making another 'retreat', a complete about-face after the watershed which was marked by his

interview with the Director of Belvedere, in the previous chapter. Therefore, because of the implications of his mother's demand on Stephen, the conflict actually runs deeper than it might seem from the surface and the tension in the passage hints at the more profound tensions within Stephen himself.

(c) Analyse the details of the passage, relating them to the opposition already noted
The passage is important in revealing this undercurrent of tension in Stephen's home life because we see nothing of it elsewhere in the chapter. But Stephen has no quarrel with his family in itself. He feels no enmity towards his father, only mocking pity perhaps, and he bears no ill-will against his mother. However, her demands on him represent what he sees as another threat to freedom and he will not permit anyone to compromise this.

The encounter with Cranly here makes it relatively easy for Joyce to show this tension because it allows Stephen to express in full his motives for denying his mother's wish. In this way Cranly also acts as an externalisation of Stephen's conscience, since he acts to make Stephen confront and reflect on his own motives. He reveals that Stephen's principle of freedom is only one reason for his denial, and that the other is Stephen's arrogant stubbornness or pride of will, typified by his declaration: 'I will not serve'. Moreover, when Cranly hints that these were the insolent words of Lucifer before his ignominious fall, its only effect is to intensify Stephen's defiance.

(d) Try to say how the passage relates to the novel as a whole
At the start of the extract Stephen reflects about himself that 'him no woman's eyes had wooed'. His failure with women is a sore point, made more acute by the recollection of Davin's tale of seduction by a peasant woman. And then, a few lines later, Stephen wonders if Cranly is 'thinking of her greeting to him under the porch', a reference to an earlier scene outside the library when Emma had greeted Cranly but ignored himself [see p. 252]. She is the same E.C. whom Stephen had wanted to kiss at the tram stop in chapter 2, and the reference here reminds us that though he continues to desire her he has still failed to woo her [see also p. 275]. In effect Stephen has failed to form any deep relationship with a girl or a woman in the novel except in terms of prostitution or through sexual fantasy. It suggests that Stephen is at ease with

women only as an idea or symbol, as the girl on the estuary in chapter 4 is, or as a form of sexual inspiration as when he composes his poem in chapter 5 to an idealised and undefined complexity of erotic shadows . . . ' lure of the fallen seraphim' [see p. 236 on]. And on the two occasions that he writes verse for Emma they really have more reference to himself than to her as expressions of romantic feeling.

He has become a defiant, ambitious, yet sad and lonely figure incapable of giving love to either female or male, and what has become his principle of rejection ultimately prevents him from forming a genuine friendship, even a tie with Cranly. His rejections of religion and family, and later of his homeland, presage a lonely future, one of denial rather than of affirmation, an existence in which he would become isolated from the very life which we would expect to be the substance of art. The dispute with his mother springs more deeply than simply from a refusal to perform his Easter duty, but more profoundly from a definition of his life which understands 'freedom' as refusal rather than engagement with the humanity which ought to be the stuff of a writer's art, and the opening sentence of the passage spotlights his aspirations in this field.

(e) Search for anything distinctive about the passage, particularly in the area of style, which you have not already noted
In spite of Cranly's claim that Stephen is an 'excitable bloody man' (though we see very little evidence in the novel to support this) the mood of this passage is cool and, on the whole, restrained. The narrator's plain discourse describing the dialogue – 'said', 'asked', 'answered' – underlines Stephen's reserve, rendering the exchange more like a dramatic catechism than a chat between friends. Because of this restraint there emerges the unmistakable suspicion that both men are aware of the imminent and inevitable demise of their friendship, and Cranly's questions have the effect of drawing out this realisation rather than effecting a change in Stephen's attitude to his family and himself. The novel's energies are winding down now towards the moment of Stephen's flight, an ebbing cadence after the emotional climax in chapter 4 and the intellectual climax of the art theory earlier in this chapter. Which is not to say that the passage lacks energy but rather that its energy emanates not from the momentum of the plot but from the tension between the two opposing positions in it, an opposition

which is typical of Joyce's approach in this chapter, with Stephen presented in a series of disputations: for example, with the Dean of Studies on language, with Davin and MacCann on art. The function of such disputations is to dramatise facets of Stephen's character, attitudes and ideas in such a way that it enables the narrator to remain almost completely concealed in the background.

(7) Have I achieved a sufficiently complex sense of the novel?

Having looked in detail at these selected passages, I think we have made good progress in understanding the pattern of the novel, as well as in getting to grips with Joyce's subtle narrative style. We have also established a reasonable view of the development of Stephen Dedalus's consciousness and attitudes, as well as of the themes and ideas which impinge on his development. But to get something like a full appreciation of Joyce's achievement in the novel we will need to think about his methods of characterisation and to see how Stephen's relationship to the reader and to the narrator alters throughout the course of the novel. In this respect, two of Joyce's chief innovations in *A Portrait* concern, on the one hand, the role of the narrator and, on the other, the special function of the epiphany, a feature which we first encountered in our discussion of *Dubliners* and so, naturally, we must examine both of these points. Also, because language plays such a crucial role in the novel, both as a subject of Stephen's development and as a key element in determining our relationship to Stephen, we must spend some time in examining Joyce's subtle linguistics.

We started our discussion of this novel by saying that its title gave us specific expectations about Stephen Dedalus's development as an artist and we must return to this issue to look at the image of the artist which is presented and in doing so to discuss the extent to which we could describe Stephen himself as an artist. We can do this by looking closely at his aesthetic theory in chapter 5 and at examples of his own writing in the novel, in particular his poem in the final chapter.

II   Aspects of the novel

When *A Portrait* first appeared in book form in 1916 it had a mixed reception. Those who were averse thought that its images of filth and sex were too vivid and too numerous, while many of the more favourable reviews focused on the unusual narrative style of the novel. It was unconventional both in terms of its images and its style and, with some bravado, Joyce was later to boast that because of this the book was rejected by every publisher in London. One publisher who did reject the manuscript complained that it was formless and 'a little sordid', while acknowledging that it was well written with vivid pictures of the life of its main character, even if the book was 'all in pieces'. The book *is* 'all in pieces' in a sense, but it can be described as 'formless' only if we come to it with rigid expectations of a conventional novel.

So, on a first reading, the novel can take us by surprise on both counts: its broken yet vivid images and also the unusual mode in which these are presented or narrated. If this is the case, then by persevering with it we can overcome its difficulties, especially as we come to realise that the pieces are held together by the presence and tensions of its chief character, Stephen Dedalus, whose point of view gives the novel a large part of its coherence. Accordingly, we may begin our further analysis, of aspects of the novel, by examining the characterisation and role of Stephen in it, especially the extent to which he gives form to this 'formless' novel.

Beginning with the title of the novel, *A Portrait of the Artist as a Young Man*, this can be seen to concentrate our attention on two key aspects of Stephen Dedalus: the artist and the young man. Joyce offers us a compelling picture of the development of the young man from his earliest memories to his departure from home and family, and before we examine the artist we should first consider the 'Young Man' and how Joyce characterises him. Two passages that will help us get started on this are taken from chapter 5, with Stephen talking to fellow students. Read them and try to assess what their themes tell us about Stephen.

– The soul is born, he said vaguely, first in those moments I told you of. It has a slow and dark birth, more mysterious than the birth of the body. When the soul of a man is born in this country there are nets flung at it to hold it back from flight. You talk to me of nationality, language, religion. I shall try to fly by those nets.

[p. 220]

– Look here, Cranly, he said. You have asked me what I would do and what I would not do. I will tell you what I will do and what I will not do. I will not serve that in which I no longer believe whether it call itself my home, my fatherland or my church: and I will try to express myself in some mode of life or art, as freely as I can and as wholly as I can, using for my defence the only arms I allow myself to use – silence, exile, and cunning.

[pp. 268–9]

It is not difficult to identify Stephen's attitude and feelings at these two points. He is, as Joyce described later, proudly 'flashing his antlers like a stag'. In addition he is urgently asserting his struggle for freedom and the two statements set out to lay claim to this. It is possible to regard Stephen's growth in the novel as his struggle for independence from the guardianship of parents, school and priests. It is a struggle through trials of injustice, traumatic shocks and insipid mediocrity, through literary experiment and heresy to a point in chapter 5 where the importance of freedom is signalled in the account of his art theory and in his verse, both paradoxically grounded in highly organised and rigorous constraints of language and form. Freedom is expressed equally in physical and intellectual terms but, while Stephen prizes freedom as the necessary adjunct of the artist, his stress is unmistakably on freedom as escape, as the first of the above passages indicates. Look again at it and note what Ireland represents for him; the very things which other people like his mother and Davin pin their faith on (for example, religion and politics) are conceived of by Stephen as obstacles to his own 'destiny'.

The second passage above refers to the 'arms' or methods which he will use to defend freedom – 'silence, exile, and cunning' – and again we can see that he has already used these throughout the course of the novel. We noted earlier how Stephen shunned children's games, happily sitting on the edge of his line or a chess match, silent and exiled. Stephen's cunning is implicit in the strategy by which he successfully escapes from Heron in chapter 2 and also in the duplicity of his attitude to sinning while still a prefect of the sodality. And do not forget that Father Dolan at Clongowes Wood detected the cunning 'schemer' in Stephen's eyes. The second passage is important also in reiterating his obstinate pride – 'I will not serve . . .' – and his endurance has been continually tested by others who have sought to make him submit or admit: Dante Riordan, Father Dolan, Mr Tate, Heron, Father Arnall, Davin and Cranly. It expresses finally his despair in his country and all its works, but we can see, too, that this obstinate pride of will has helped him to withstand the knocks, bullyings, humiliations and trials and to have come through, until in the final chapters he has the strength to set out his own vision, or at least part of it.

Setting out this vision is a marker for Stephen's intellectual development. Stephen does not make it very clear why he considers it necessary to be free in such an extreme sense, but he gives the impression that he feels this is necessary in order to creatively express his unique selfhood. To do this he must explore his intellectual and artistic potential to their limits. This possibility can be seen in early chapters in Stephen's acute attentiveness to sense experiences, his preoccupation with words, puns and verbal riddles, the sounds of words and in particular their relationship to reality. He writes verses about Parnell and the tram episode, wins a prize for one essay and is scandalised for heresy in another; he is chastised by Heron for his unconventional tastes in literature. Intellectually he is marked above the rest of his peers in chapter 1, where he regularly achieves first place in 'elements' at Clongowes Wood, and he has some dizzying speculations about the universe (with himself at its centre, of course) and theology. These early distinctions are sustained in subsequent chapters, eventually overcoming even the setbacks in chapter 3, and Stephen's intellectual development reaches its climax in the metaphysics of his art theory in chapter 5.

This concentration on internal states is Joyce's chief method of characterisation in *A Portrait*. Even when he deals with external actions or settings they are invariably the window onto mental states, especially in revealing to the reader the extent of Stephen's development (for example, see how Joyce makes the events on pages 186 and 245 reflect on Stephen's internal growth). This is very much the method by which Joyce reveals how early experiences have a deep effect on character. But, further, these experiences are often repeated later in a different form, and ultimately become the stuff of art for Stephen (for example, the villanelle in chapter 5 uses the seduction motif which occurs in chapter 2 in the forms of Mercedes and the prostitute). Stephen is frequently presented in such archetypal situations at different stages of his life, and Joyce again marks the subtle changes in internal states by the ways in which Stephen deals with them.

A good example of this is a comparison of Stephen's interview in chapter 1 with Father Conmee and his interview with the Director of Belvedere in chapter 4. A brief extract from each will help to make this clearer.

He saw the rector sitting at a desk writing. There was a skull on the desk and a strange solemn smell in the room like the old leather of chairs.

His heart was beating fast on account of the solemn place he was in and the silence of the room: and he looked at the skull and at the rector's kindlooking face.

– Well, my little man, said the rector, what is it?

[p. 58]

The priest's face was in total shadow but the waning daylight from behind him touched the deeply grooved temples and the curves of the skull. Stephen followed also with his ears the accents and intervals of the priest's voice as he spoke gravely and cordially of indifferent themes, the vacation which had just ended, the colleges of the order abroad, the transference of masters. The grave and cordial voice went on easily with its tale, and in the pauses Stephen felt bound to set it on again with respectful questions. He knew that the tale was a prelude and his mind waited for the sequel.

[pp. 166–7]

It is, of course, no accident that a skull appears in each episode, signalling the comparison to be made between the two. The differences between the two are equally clear: in the first, Stephen is intimidated by the occasion and the solemnity of the office; in the second, he is distant from the 'voice and the tale', patronising the Director with his 'respectful questions'. The differences are made more explicit when Stephen later reflects on the Director's invitation to the priesthood, and Stephen's subsequent rejection of this reveals that he has at last managed to overcome the awesome presence of the Church (compare these also with the scene in chapter 5 when Stephen lectures the Dean on the language of philosophy).

Consider, too, Joyce's language in these two passages and try to see how it affects our view of Stephen in them. Have a look at the vocabulary in each and decide what it says about him. Also, you will notice a difference even in the lengths of the sentences in each extract: what does it reveal about Stephen's mood and attitude to the priests in each?

In the first passage Stephen's response to the situation is emotional and intense; in the second, his response is intellectual and dispassionate. The differences in the vocabulary are manifest, too: the simple diction of the first stresses surface and material features, with the repetition of 'and' hinting at the breathlessness of the small boy, whereas that in the second embodies a complex interchange between the setting, the director's subject matter and Stephen's response to it (and a hint of irony in the repetition of the words 'grave and cordial'). Such differences are also to be found in the sentence structures: the first has simple constructions, loose and transparent that appear spontaneous; the second has more complex, but slightly tired symmetries.

The differences noted, however, are crucial for, throughout the novel, Joyce's modulation of styles in this way is a key device in his characterisation of Stephen: at each stage Stephen's internal development is paralleled by a sequence of increasingly maturing styles of language. This was one of Joyce's revolutionary innovations in the novel and seems to have come about as a result of his tremendous flair for parody and pastiche, writing each section in a style appropriate to each stage of Stephen's 'progress'. So, the opening pages are presented in a register intending to suggest infancy; parts of chapter 2 are in a romantic style appropriate to Stephen's own reading as well as to his drive to escape through the imagination; and then the style of the second passage above resembles that of Joyce's favourite prose writer Cardinal Newman; finally, the dialogue in which Stephen reveals his art theory in chapter 5 recalls another of Joyce's favourite writers, the dramatist Ibsen, and when Stephen begins to compose his villanelle the idiom of the narrator recalls that of the art critic John Ruskin.

At the same time we can note that because the style of the language changes there is no single viewpoint as we read through the book; for instance, we do not particularly feel that it is written wholly from an adult's point of view. Each stage is experienced through an increasingly mature viewpoint (yet by the end an impression lingers that Stephen has still not yet achieved for himself a fully mature style, a point which is implied by the fragmentation in the diaries). And because of this modulation in the styles we do not become aware of the identity of the originator of them, the narrator – which is the next important topic for our discussion.

At the outset we can say that the narrator is not Stephen himself. Nor is it Joyce. But if we consider it more carefully we can see that it is really a matrix of both, of Stephen's developing consciousness and Joyce's overall arrangement and form. However, in Joyce's first version of the novel, he adopted a more conventional, omniscient narrator with a conventional retrospective point of view. This not only presented events but also commented on Stephen's actions and inner states. Joyce later became thoroughly dissatisfied with this first attempt, which had the working title *Stephen Hero*, and even attempted to destroy the manuscript by flinging it in the fire. It was rescued, and the remaining parts (some 250 pages) were published after Joyce's death. *Stephen Hero* gives some interesting insights into the style of *A Portrait*.

One of these is that while in *Stephen Hero* events run fluently, conventionally, one from another, in *A Portrait* episodes are frequently truncated, left suspended in silence. On first publication of the novel, one reviewer complained about this feature, saying that its 'kinematographic effects' led to a lack of clarity; he added that although Joyce was a clever and skilful artist 'it is all objectively viewed and objectively rendered, the character has no continuum, no personality . . . [Joyce] keeps to the circumference of his hero's mind, and never drives to the centre of his soul'. I think, however, that we can agree with only part of this. The reference to cinematic effects (as we would probably now call them) relates, of course, to Joyce's method of giving us only fragments of experience, events, dreams and emotions, and on a first reading the shock-effect of these can lead to confusion and a lack of clarity. But the novel was something new for its time, and its devices – made necessary by Joyce's overall aims – make demands on the reader's efforts not previously made in literature. To appreciate, this as well as Joyce's aims, we would need to consider briefly how the narrative of *A Portrait* differs from what went before it, especially the nineteenth-century novel.

If we were to enquire what gives earlier novels their greater clarity – works such as, say, Thomas Hardy's *Tess of the D'Urbevilles* or George Eliot's *The Mill on the Floss* – then we could begin by examining the role and characteristics of the narrator in each novel. In these works the narrator acts as an intermediary between the experiences of the character and the reader. The narrator intervenes, often interpreting as well as describing events, and commenting freely and directly on the mortality of the characters. Through this intervening discourse, the narrator acts as the mouthpiece of the author and as a guide to the reader, controlling both the narrative and the reader's response, imposing a view of the events from outside of them. In this way, in the act of clarifying the text the narrator ironically acts as much as a barrier as a window.

Let us look closely at a passage from *A Portrait* to see how it differs:

> It would be nice to lie on the hearthrug before the fire, leaning his head upon

his hands, and think on those sentences. He shivered as if he had cold slimy water next his skin. That was mean of Wells to shoulder him into the square ditch because he would not swop his little snuffbox for Wells's seasoned hacking chestnut, the conqueror of forty. How cold and slimy the water had been! A fellow had once seen a big rat jump into the scum. Mother was sitting at the fire with Dante waiting for Brigid to bring in the tea. She had her feet on the fender and her jewelly slippers were so hot and they had such a lovely warm smell! Dante knew a lot of things. She had taught him where the Mozambique Channel was and what was the longest river in America and what was the name of the highest mountain in the moon. Father Arnall knew more than Dante because he was a priest but both his father and uncle Charles said that Dante was a clever woman and a wellread woman. And when Dante made that noise after dinner and then put her hand up to her mouth: that was heartburn.

[p. 7]

Clearly this is not the point of view of the narrator, even though the narration uses the third person – 'he shivered' rather than 'I shivered'. We can see without much difficulty that the thoughts are those of Stephen, presented in close proximity to the reader. They are also presented in Stephen's own immature idiom; for instance, the two words 'nice' and 'mean' can be recognised as the two chief principles of Stephen's moral responses throughout chapter 1. There is a chain of widely diverse images, which is also typical of Stephen's divergent thought pattern, as is his tendency to reveal his own sense-impressions of external events – heat and cold, a warm smell, a strange noise. His immature perspective strives to make order of his world through the agency of adults who are important to him (Father Arnall takes over here from Dante as the more knowledgeable authority), but it is his own viewpoint which creates the comic effect at the end. There is no obvious narrative discourse, the narrator does not intervene to comment on Wells (it is, of course, Stephen who describes him as 'mean') or to comment on Stephen (though the comic effect at the end does this for him). All of which means that it is left to the reader to do these.

Try this type of analysis for yourself on other passages from the novel and you will achieve a more thorough understanding of the relationship between the narrator and the text as well as of Joyce's methods. Our conclusions above will hold good for the rest of the novel. For example, Joyce's narrator does not make any explicit moral comments about Stephen's visits to the prostitutes, or about his attitude to family and friends. The narrator's discourse exists only in the selection and arrangement of material, and because Joyce uses the filter of Stephen's consciousness to communicate experience at different ages this selection and arrangement are made to appear to be Stephen's own. This technique, of the narrator using the character's point of point but still remaining outside that character, is a refinement of that device which we met in *Dubliners*, now usually called 'free indirect style'. So, referring to the above passage, although I said that the images are diverse, the thing which holds them together is Stephen's mind. Thus, in spite of the early critic's misgivings, we do in a vivid sense drive 'close to the centre of his soul'.

But if, I hear you ask, Joyce wanted to drive close to the soul, why didn't he use a first-person narrator? Well, perhaps it would work, but the chief disadvantage of the first-person mode is that to achieve a moral awareness the central character would need to be continually reflecting on his/her actions; the 'I' consciousness would have to be constantly and oppressively self-conscious. Joyce's free indirect style in *A Portrait* allows him to control the point of view and the emotional intensity more subtly while at the same time retaining something of the intimacy of an 'I' narration. Equally, while Joyce does not intrude any direct moral commentary of his own, he may be able to comment indirectly through the selection and arrangement, as we will observe below.

In terms of form, too, *A Portrait* marks a new direction for Joyce as a result of the renewed prominence he gave to the role of the epiphany in his writing. As it was in *Dubliners*, the epiphany is the central vehicle for conveying the experiences of the novel, but now Joyce also employs it as the chief structural principle of the narrative. This fits in with Joyce's shift in attention to inner states in the novel. And yet, while it has such an important function in *A Portrait*, he nowhere refers to it in the novel, and for a definition of the concept we have to look at *Stephen Hero*. There, in chapter XXV, as Stephen explains his aesthetic theory to an apathetic Cranly, he tries to describe the process of seeing into the reality of an experience: 'By an epiphany he meant a sudden spiritual manifestation, whether in the vulgarity of speech or in a memorable phase of the mind itself.' He proceeds to expand on this by saying that even a simple, everyday thing such as a clock on a building can be the object of an epiphany:

> – Yes, said Stephen. I will pass it time after time, allude to it refer to it, catch a glimpse of it. It is only an item in the catalogue of Dublin's street furniture. Then

all at once I see it and I know what it is: epiphany.
  – What?
  – Imagine my glimpses at that clock as the gropings of a spiritual eye which seeks to adjust its vision to an exact focus. The moment the focus is reached the object is epiphanised. It is just in this epiphany that I find the third, the supreme quality of beauty.

[*Stephen Hero* (Granada, 1977) p. 189]

For Stephen, then, an epiphany is a sudden insight into truth or beauty. By saying that the spiritual eye might 'adjust its vision to an exact focus' he shows that 'epiphany' refers to a change in the observer; a 'spiritual manifestation' marks a realisation by the observer rather than any change in the object of perception – as Stephen explains, it is a 'memorable phase of the *mind*'. His use of the words 'sudden' and 'evanescent' indicates the fleetingness of the state.

We can thus understand an epiphany as a heightened manifestation of the reality of even some everyday occurrence (what Stephen in *A Portrait* calls its *quidditas*). A good example of this from the novel is the epiphany in chapter 4, discussed above, in which Stephen, returning home after the interview with the Director of Belvedere, finds in the squalor of his kitchen a sort of affirmation of his decision to reject the priesthood [p. 176; at the end of the novel the diary entries for 25 March, 10 April and 16 April also provide good examples]. Elsewhere, however, the significance of an epiphany may not be made explicit for the reader: for example, what can we make of the 'Mabel Hunter' epiphany on page 70? or of the 'foetus' epiphany on the trip to Queen's College, on page 95?

So we can begin to see, I hope, that an epiphany has a number of important aspects. For Joyce as for Stephen it is the process by which we may suddenly apprehend the hidden truth of even some ordinary event, by which the everyday is transmuted into a profound experience, an evanescent moment of heightened reality, and often a mystical one whose significance is sometimes unclear but which offers a sacramental insight; a timeless moment in time. In addition, it is also the essential and elusive quality of beauty in art, *quidditas*. Further, in *Stephen Hero* Stephen asserts that it is the responsibility of the artist, the 'man of letters', to meticulously record these epiphanies, and this is exactly what Joyce himself did, his notes becoming the substance of his fictional writings (it may be for this reason, that some of the epiphanies in *A Portrait* are obscure, since they sometimes appear to have only private significance for Joyce himself).

In this way the epiphany plays a central role in Joyce's fiction since it is employed as a naturalistic method of revealing events to the reader. Thus what we have in *A Portrait* is a complex sequence of epiphanies ordered through Stephen's consciousness, arranged not in terms of their chronological occurrence (as we might expect of a conventional biographical novel) but in terms of their priority for Stephen himself.

The concept of epiphany has important implications for Stephen's art theory, too. In chapter 5 Stephen draws an implicit parallel between the process by which the reality of an everyday object is manifested and the process by which the beauty of an object is revealed. He sets this out in his lecture on aesthetics to Lynch when he uses the Latin term *claritas*, or 'radiance', to describe the supreme essence of beauty. It is a masterful theory but it is not at first easy to follow, and yet it is not important to understand all its details. So, you may wonder, why is it there at all? One reason is that it does tell us quite a lot about Stephen himself, and another is that the emphases in it bear on Stephen's progress as an artist: we can see what he means by 'artist' and appraise him by his own criteria as well as by ours. Hence we will begin a survey of his theory with these two points clearly in mind.

The structure of the art theory in chapter 5 can be divided, roughly speaking, into three parts. The first [pp. 221–6] presents some intellectual reflections on terror and pity, as well as a general background to a basic aesthetic question: namely, why do different people find different things beautiful? He explains that he is interested only in artistic, man-made beauty rather than natural objects or Lynch's animalistic impulses. Next [pp. 227–31] he sets out to define the basic universal prerequisites of artificial beauty, using St Thomas Aquinas as his starting point. These are wholeness (*integritas*), harmony (*consonantia*), radiance (*claritas*), and while he finds the first two relatively simple to explain he gets stuck on the third and must use spiritual metaphors to imply the state of mind of the beholder (rather than something in the object), with the expressions 'luminous silent stasis' and an 'enchantment of the heart'. Stephen concludes his account [pp. 232–3] with definitions of three literary forms – lyrical, epical and dramatic – defined according to the degree to which the artist is present in the work of art.

What then does all this reveal of Stephen? For one thing it reveals by how much he has advanced intellectually since his epiphany at the end of chapter 4. We see, too, that his interest in art is serious and that he is resolute about it; we are convinced that he has dedicated himself to art, and in a book in which Stephen rejects so much we should not overlook the importance of this point. It is a strong, very persuasive theory of 'art for art's sake', displaying not only Stephen's assured competency with some of the key ideas in the field of aesthetics (those of Aristotle, Aquinas, Lessing and Goethe), but also his readiness to conceptualise and to synthesise his own ideas. It represents the intellectual climax of the novel (as the estuary epiphany represented the emotional one). At the same time his lecture to Lynch (like the earlier lecture to the Dean) reveals how much he has cast himself in the role of the 'farcical pedagogue' which he parodied in the Belvedere concert in chapter 2. His assertiveness here not only betrays pride in his own ability but also gives the impression now of certainty amid so much that is deferred or obfuscated.

However, the excrement-eating and buttock-scribbling Lynch is a meagre audience, passive, complaisant and offering little in the way of constructive comment. Stephen lacks a worthy audience and this encourages him to turn inward, to abstract and to intellectualise, and this further isolates him from his fellow students. At the same time, few seem eager to seek his friendship. The art theory tells us what a clever, wholly dedicated young man he has become but also what a coldly rational one, preoccupied with form in art and with analytics in thought. And Joyce positions the theory just before Stephen's own poetic composition [pp. 242–3], giving us the chance to see the theory in action and, inevitably, to judge the poem against the theory.

Is it a good poem? This is an important question, not only for the reasons just given but also because it will help us decide on another question, raised by the title: is Stephen really an artist? It might seem a little odd to ask this question, but the internal case for supposing Stephen to be an artist rests almost exclusively on the evidence in the villanelle composed in chapter 5. The Dean at university calls him an artist, 'You are an artist, are you not, Mr Dedalus?' [p. 200], although Cranly derides him with 'You poor poet, you!' [p. 269]. Stephen himself has had a strong conviction about his destiny, at least since the close of chapter 4, but by the end of chapter 5 he has become uncertain as he faces a future in which the emphasis is on escape.

The poem itself, a villanelle, has had a more divisive effect on critics than any other single aspect of the novel. We need to examine it more closely:

> Are you not weary of ardent ways,
> Lure of the fallen seraphim?
> Tell no more of enchanted days.
>
> Your eyes have set man's heart ablaze
> And you have had your will of him.
> Are you not weary of ardent ways?
>
> Above the flame the smoke of praise
> Goes up from ocean rim to rim.
> Tell no more of enchanted days.
>
> Our broken cries and mournful lays
> Rise in one eucharistic hymn.
> Are you not weary of ardent ways?
>
> While sacrificing hands upraise
> The chalice flowing to the brim,
> Tell no more of enchanted days.
>
> And still you hold our longing gaze
> With languorous look and lavish limb!
> Are you not weary of ardent ways?
> Tell no more of enchanted days.

The mood of the poem maintains that air of warmth and languid mystery of the narrative which leads up to its composition and it coheres exactly with the sensuous prose in which this section is narrated. It appears to emerge from an erotic fantasy, probably concerning E.C. again ('He had written verses for her again after ten years' [p. 241]),echoing those verses written after the tram episode in chapter 2, and also recalling the erotic material for which Stephen had such pangs of shame in chapter 3. And like that early verse the setting is abstracted away in favour of the 'undefined sorrow' which rules it. Its subject, a shadowy seductress, is elusive and the 'poet' adopts a romanticised posture of the abandoned lover. The absence of detail or of any focused emotion limits it as public utterance since it is difficult to share whatever is happening, while its very tightly controlled maze of idea and sound has the effect of mesmerising rather than moving the reader. In spite of its emotional diction (cries, mournful, longing) it is devoid of any accessible emotion, and its principal achievement is the mastery of a difficult, convoluted verse form.

For these reasons, the lyric comes across to me as an impersonal production, an exercise in composition rather than as a verse sprung from some deep well of emotion, and its importance relies more on its position and its role in the novel in relation to Stephen than on its merits as a free-standing composition. In this respect it ties in with a general despondency in Stephen at this stage in his life, encapsulating his failure to respond to or reach the opposite sex (in particular E.C., of course) except on formalised terms which regards them as either unapproachable virgin or temptress-whore. It tends to confirm that impression given by the aesthetic theory, that he has become a highly intellectualised individual, preoccupied with form and order rather than with feeling and humanity (in this respect compare him with James Duffy in 'A Painful Case', who like Stephen is described as a 'shy guest at the feast of the world's culture' [*A Portrait*, p. 194]).

Against this we can say that it does reveal Stephen's commitment to his 'destiny' as well as his mastery of the skill and discipline of his craft. It is the work of an apprentice rather than a mature production. At the same point in his own life, Joyce's verse was in general equally feeble, at best notable chiefly for its formal and verbal dexterity, its mysterious atmospheres and obscure moods. It is, of course, possible to apply the same conclusions to Stephen's piece, and for this reason we can say that the poem is important in what it tells us about Stephen as an individual and as aspiring artist, and so we can regard it in the same way as we regard the aesthetic theory, more as a pointer than as a proof of ability.

The villanelle, then, is the principal feature by which we can measure Stephen's development as an artist. But it is not the only evidence. From an early age there are clear indications of Stephen's disposition towards art, and the primacy for him of art over life:

> Words which he did not understand he said over and over to himself till he had learned them by heart: and through them he had glimpses of the real world about him.
>
> [p. 64]

and on the estuary, in chapter 4:

> – A day of dappled seaborn clouds.
> The phrase and the day and the scene harmonised in a chord. Words. Was it their colours? He allowed them to glow and fade, hue after hue: sunrise gold, the russet and green of apple orchards, azure of waves, the greyfringed fleece of clouds. No, it was not their colours: it was the poise and balance of the period itself. Did he then love the rhythmic rise and fall of words better than their associations of legend and colour? Or was it that, being as weak of sight as he was shy of mind, he drew less pleasure from the reflection of the glowing sensible world through the prism of language many coloured and richly storied than from the contemplation of an inner world of individual emotions mirrored perfectly in a lucid supple periodic prose?
>
> [p. 181]

This does not prove that he is an artist, of course, only that he is sensitive to the musicality and sorcery of words. On the other hand, after the fourth chapter Stephen himself is convinced of his own destiny, and in the moment of composition of his verse he figures himself as an artist, a 'priest of eternal imagination, transmuting the daily bread of experience into the radiant body of everliving life' [p. 240]. By equating the artist with the priest Stephen also confers a mystical dimension on the role of the artist as an attempt to account for the mysterious process by which art is inspired. The same mysticism is envisaged when he evokes the myth of Daedalus (the 'hawklike man whose name he bore' [p. 244]), the cunning artificer and designer of the maze (which can be seen as symbol of art but, significantly too, of form and order). By comparing the artist to the priest Stephen also suggests that the artist's is a spiritual vocation, and Joyce makes this more explicit by having the important epiphany on the estuary follow on immediately from Stephen's rejection of the Director's 'offer' of the Catholic priesthood in chapter 4. It is another aspect of what can be called a sacramental vision of art, one which makes the role of the artist akin to that of a high priest, and it includes too the mystical working of the epiphany, a semi-divine moment of insight.

Having apprehended his vocation, Stephen embraces it resolutely and dedicates himself to its providence. We might even say that he submits himself to it, as the acolyte described by Stephen in chapter 4 [see p. 172]. And this is where the problem begins in assessing Stephen as an artist. He takes up the role of the artist as yet another posture or guise, and in composing the villanelle he seems to relish the part. It promises fulfilment and reflects well on self-esteem rather than offering a mode of expression particularly; in other words the role of artist gives him a sense of identity (remember, too, that after writing the tram-stop verses Stephen 'gazed at his face for a long time in the mirror' [p. 74]). This is supported by the principle underpinning his aesthetic theory, of 'art for art's sake': the work of art finds its justification within himself, not in whether or not it communicates anything to anyone else. For him art is a form of self-expression. As the book proceeds he makes less and less direct contact with other people, until, by the close, the only person he communicates with is himself – symbolised by the diary, a self-referencing form for private consumption. Furthermore, although Stephen's ultimate intention is to go forth and encounter the 'reality of experience', and to transmute this life into art, what we actually see in practice is an individual withdrawing from direct experience to live life at one stage removed.

Does Joyce himself offer any clues to the question of whether Stephen is or will become an artist? One way to consider this is to examine Joyce's relationship to his main character. We can begin by saying that for much of the first part of the novel Joyce presents Stephen with some sympathy: his weaknesses and folly are those of childhood, and the vulnerable style of the opening chapters mirrors this. Yet in the final chapter the point of view is different, with Joyce more distinctly ironic towards Stephen, who is presented now as a clever man but, underneath, aloof, loveless and misguided, rejecting petitions, lecturing the dean and his friends on an art theory devoid of feeling, posturing as an aesthete, and ultimately rejecting the love of his mother. In the final pages, the diaries present to us a picture of a disembodied consciousness, cut off from life, reminding us of Stephen's own God of creation 'behind or beyond or above . . . refined out of existence, indifferent' [p. 233]. He cuts a sad, isolated figure. His call of 'Welcome, O life!' on the penultimate page could otherwise seem a triumphant embrace but for the irony of his situation and his single-minded thrust to deny, to reject, to seek exile and silence.

The last sentence of the novel is a prayer to his eponymous hero-spirit, 'Old father, old artificer . . . ', but is Stephen to soar like Daedalus, the archetypal artist, or is he instead doomed to crash like the proud, overreaching Icarus? His prayer expresses his own uncertainty, and of course ours. By the close we cannot say with any certainty that Stephen is an artist and, ending where it does, the novel puts us into something of the same position as Stephen himself, unaware of what the future holds for him. The motto to the novel is important here, too, underlining this ignorance: it comes from Ovid's account of Daedalus as he is about to construct the famous waxen wings: *Et ignotas animum dimittit in artes* – 'and he set his mind to explore unknown arts' [p. 1]. But we are not in exactly the same position as Stephen because Joyce's irony has allowed us to see more of Stephen than Stephen sees of himself, and it is this irony which makes us hesitate in acclaiming him as an artist. All we can realistically conclude is that he is an aspiring, potential, artist. He will realise his ambition only if he can come to terms with his pride and his want of feeling. As he is now, he is in no position to 'forge' the conscience of his race because his own conscience is itself so unformed. As his mother says, he must learn in his own life, and away from home, what the heart is and what it feels.

4

Ulysses: 'in the heart of the hibernian metropolis'

I Constructing an overall analysis

ULYSSES is James Joyce's masterpiece, and it is without doubt the most important novel of the twentieth century. After *A Portrait*, it marks a great leap forward, a revolution in the novel, and its impact continues to resound today, over seventy years since its first publication. Originally conceived by Joyce as an additional *Dubliners* story, *Ulysses* looks back to the short stories for its settings and themes, and for some of its innumerable characters, but it does so as part of a new epic and heroic vision.

A brief summary of the plot will reveal the outline form of the novel and at the same time perhaps suggest some familiar features to those who have already read *Dubliners*.

(1) After reading the novel think about the story and what kind of pattern you can see in the text

The narrative of *Ulysses* concerns among (many) other matters the roamings across Dublin of its two chief characters, Stephen Dedalus and Leopold Bloom, throughout a single day: Thursday, the 16th of June, 1904. These begin as two separate strands, which eventually converge, and the plot of the novel is very simply the story of how the paths of these two strands cross and for a time merge together.

Stephen's day begins in a Martello tower on the edge of Dublin where he is temporarily lodging after his return from Paris. He is uneasy with the tower's two other residents and Stephen decides to quit the tower for good. For the past three weeks he has been working as a schoolteacher in Dalkey and although he is unhappy in his post the pupils are stimulated by his droll puzzles and his

lack of discipline. The headmaster, a bigoted anti-Semitic Orange-
man, hands him his pay and a lecture on history and then asks
Stephen for his help in getting a letter into the Irish press. It is a
day for decisions and, as Stephen will later explain, he quits his
job today too. We see him next on the beach at Sandymount,
alone, brooding moodily on his present life and his lofty failed
ambitions, aware that his life has become as formless as the sea
and as inert as the heavy sands beneath his feet. A nightmare
vision of his dead mother warns him of his loveless existence and,
while he makes no positive gesture towards amending it, he
receives a mysterious intuition that its course is about to change in
some momentous encounter. He sets out to greet it.

In the fourth chapter the novel switches attention to the home of
Leopold Bloom, married man, father of Milly, canvasser of advertisements, part-Jew, part-Gentile, an all-round man with a touch of
the artist about him, a dark horse and a scapegoat. Unlike Stephen,
Mr Bloom lives in the heart of the Dublin metropolis and his dealings are enmeshed in the lives of his fellow citizens. His story begins
in his home at 7 Eccles Street, serving breakfast in bed to his wife
Molly with a letter from 'Blazes' Boylan, a tenor with whom she is
preparing to make a singing tour of Ireland. Mr Bloom leaves
home, and after picking up a letter downtown, he orders Molly's
ointment at a chemist and then bumps into Bantam Lyons, an
acquaintance. In their idle conversation Lyons mistakes a remark
by Mr Bloom as a tip for the Gold Cup, the big race of the day, a
mistake that will have very painful consequences for Bloom.

Another friend of Mr Bloom's, Patrick Dignam, has recently
died and at his funeral later in the morning an indiscreet comment from one of the mourners reminds Mr Bloom that it is
almost the anniversary of his father's suicide. He reflects, too, on
the death of his only son, Rudy, who had died soon after his birth.
Mr Bloom feels stultified by these thoughts of death, surrounded
by the shades of Glasnevin Cemetery, and decides to return to the
living of Dublin. However, Mr Bloom is most often ostracised by
his fellow citizens, such as when he calls at the newspaper offices
in chapter 7 where, in contrast to the welcome extended there to
Stephen Dedalus, he is mocked and rebuffed. In fact the central
chapters of the novel emphasise this impression of his alienation
amidst the teeming life of the city.

In these middle chapters, Mr Bloom encounters a series of Dublin characters: twice he almost meets Stephen Dedalus, then

bumps into a former girlfriend, Josie Breen, a lunatic, Parnell's brother, a famous poet, Bob Doran, Nosey Flynn, a blind stripling, Blazes Boylan, a lawyer, Mr Dedalus and a racist. Many of the people he meets also set off in his mind the major preoccupation of his day – Molly's adulterous assignation with Boylan in the afternoon – and this triggers off memories of the past such as Mr Bloom's first meeting with Molly, and the picnic at Howth when she agreed to marry him. Such thoughts intensify the barrier between the indefatigable life of Bloom's mind and the harsh urban realities of Dublin and this further increases our sense of his isolation.

As his anguish increases, Mr Bloom takes refuge in the Ormond Bar but is devastated by the arrival at about 4 o'clock of Blazes Boylan, *en route* to Molly, and he leaves for his appointment with Martin Cunningham at Barney Kiernan's pub. Here he is again the victim of suspicion and rumour and after making a stand for persecuted Jews he is violently attacked by a one-eyed racist. He escapes and finds some relief on the beach at Sandymount, before setting off for the Holles Street maternity hospital where Mrs Purefoy has been in labour for three days. At the hospital he meets Stephen Dedalus, whose drunken friends are hotly discussing the ethics of debauchery and contraception, until the birth of Mrs Purefoy's son is announced and the whole company spews out in a drunken riot, heading for nearby Burke's bar.

In one of the strangest chapters of the novel, Mr Bloom pursues Stephen through Dublin's brothel district, Nighttown. But, while we witness Stephen's dizzy confrontations with prostitutes and soldiers, the chapter focuses chiefly on the fears, illusions, themes and people that have haunted Bloom throughout his day, now re-hashed and filtered through the trauma of Molly's infidelity. At the end of a series of surrealistic adventures he is bullied and humiliated by Bella Cohen, whore-mistress, and the novel reaches its emotional climax when he and Stephen are projected in a mystical relationship and Stephen shatters a chandelier with his ashplant. The frenzied episode gradually dissolves into order once more after Stephen is thumped to the ground by a British soldier. Mr Bloom rescues him and takes him first to a cabman's shelter and then back to Mr Bloom's home where Stephen declines the offer of accommodation though agreeing to meet again in the future. Stephen departs, leaving Mr Bloom to come to terms with his wife's infidelity.

As he retires to bed he wakes Molly and the final chapter begins with an intensely crowded stream of thoughts, in which Molly reflects on the broad panorama of her life, its desires and realities, her lovers and admirers, her youth in Gibraltar and her married life with Mr Bloom. In her thoughts, Bloom eventually triumphs over Boylan and the book closes with her climactic vision of the day on Howth Hill when she agreed to marry him, her final word ('yes') resonating beyond the end of the novel, symbolically affirming life and return.

This is, of course, an extremely simplified version of the novel, reduced to a few surface events, but although you (or I for that matter) may not apprehend all of its details, the plot of *Ulysses* is indeed a very simple, even an ordinary one: a day in the life of an ordinary, middle-aged citizen who wanders around Dublin and meets a young drifter with aspirations of becoming an artist. But, clearly, *Ulysses* is more than this, far more than its 'story', and even in my simplistic description there is a hint of the deeper significances of the story; for example, in the encounter of Bloom the citizen and Stephen the artist there is a discovery of what each may represent for the fuller realisation of the other. It is also a tale told of a father in search of a son and a son in search of a father, two lines that point to one of the central issues of Joyce's work as a whole – the family, its nature and its complex life. Stephen's fixation on his dead mother and on the absent father clearly relates to this theme, while Molly Bloom's afternoon liaison with Boylan provokes acute moral questions about the family. That Joyce chose to set the novel in his native Dublin rather than his adopted Zurich or Paris naturally draws our attention to the political and religious problems of Ireland – problems as relevant today as they were when the book was first published in 1922. The lives and backgrounds of both Mr Bloom and Stephen Dedalus provoke important racial issues, too, and the novel has frequent reminders of the imperial theme, of both Roman and British empires.

Already, perhaps, you have begun to grapple with the elaborate universe of this brilliant novel, Joyce's comic masterpiece, with its subtly interwoven threads and its radical experiments in style and language. At heart it is a novel of wandering and return, not simply for its characters but for us too, its readers, since if we are to approach anywhere near an understanding of it we will need to re-read it many times. Let us begin our detailed analysis of this book of many happy returns by making a careful analysis of some selected passages from it.

(2) Select a short passage from early in the novel and try to build upon the ideas you have established so far

I have decided to take a look at a passage from the early pages of the opening chapter of the novel. Stephen Dedalus has been summoned to the parapet of the Martello tower by his companion, the mercurial Buck Mulligan who is having a shave. He is impervious to Stephen's moody brooding.

> He came over to the gunrest and, thrusting a hand into Stephen's upper pocket, said:
> – Lend us a loan of your noserag to wipe my razor.
> Stephen suffered him to pull out and hold up on show by its corner a dirty crumpled handkerchief. Buck Mulligan wiped the razorblade neatly. Then, gazing over the handkerchief, he said:
> – The bard's noserag. A new art colour for our Irish poets: snotgreen. You can almost taste it, can't you?
> He mounted to the parapet again and gazed out over Dublin bay, his fair oakpale hair stirring slightly.
> – God, he said quietly. Isn't the sea what Algy calls it: a grey sweet mother? The snotgreen sea. The scrotumtightening sea. *Epi oinopa ponton.* Ah, Dedalus, the Greeks. I must teach you. You must read them in the original. *Thalatta! Thalatta!* She is our great sweet mother. Come and look.
> Stephen stood up and went over to the parapet. Leaning on it he looked down on the water and on the mailboat clearing the harbour mouth of Kingstown.
> – Our mighty mother, Buck Mulligan said.
> He turned abruptly his great searching eyes from the sea to Stephen's face.
> – The aunt thinks you killed your mother, he said. That's why she wont't let me have anything to do with you.
> – Someone killed her, Stephen said, gloomily.
> – You could have knelt down, damn it, Kinch, when your dying mother asked you, Buck Mulligan said. I'm hyperborean as much as you. But to think of your mother begging you with her last breath to kneel down and pray for her. And you refused. There is something sinister in you . . .
> He broke off and lathered again lightly his farther cheek. A tolerant smile curled his lips.
> – But a lovely mummer, he murmured to himself. Kinch the loveliest mummer of them all.
> He shaved evenly and with care, in silence, seriously.
> Stephen, an elbow rested on the jagged granite, leaned his palm against his brow and gazed at the fraying edge of his shiny black coat-sleeve. Pain that was not

yet the pain of love, fretted his heart. Silently, in a dream she had come to him after her death, her wasted body within its loose graveclothes giving off an odour of wax and rosewood, her breath, that had bent upon him, mute reproachful, a faint odour of wetted ashes. Across the threadbare cuffedge he saw the sea hailed as a great sweet mother by the wellfed voice beside him. The ring of bay and skyline held a dull green mass of liquid. A bowl of white china had stood beside her deathbed holding the green sluggish bile which she had torn up from her rotting liver by fits of loud groaning vomiting.

[*Ulysses* (Penguin, 1992) pp. 3–4]

In discussing this and other passages from *Ulysses* I will use the same plan as I used in my previous chapter but without setting out each of the stages of it. So let us begin by asking what the passage is about. In simple terms, Stephen Dedalus, whom we met in *A Portrait*, has returned from Paris disillusioned with his ambitions and uncertain about his future. It is early morning and a fresh, self-assured Buck Mulligan taunts him and exploits his uncertainty and passiveness. His gibe about the death of Stephen's mother injects some tension into the passage, striking a raw nerve in his listener's conscience because although Stephen killed his mother neither literally nor metaphorically, Mulligan does remind him of his dispassionate treatment of her. The vivid dream-image of Stephen's mother haunts his waking life and holds him in its thrall.

The final paragraph in the passage marks a pregnant silence in the exchange between Mulligan and Stephen during which Mulligan's words reverberate poignantly. They seem to emulate the voice of Stephen's own conscience and Stephen's response is equally vivid, with its dramatic picture of his dying mother vomiting into a bowl. It is as if Stephen finds some relief in the exaggeration of these ideas since by intensifying them in this way they form a sort of expiation for him. Mulligan, on the other hand, takes fiendish delight in annoying Stephen. His taunts are as incisive as his description of Stephen's begging mother is melodramatic. He is indifferent, of course, to Stephen's suffering and continues shaving, while his 'tolerant smile' hints at the pleasure he takes from this baiting. Furthermore, his description of Stephen as a 'mummer' implies that he is like an actor, coldly playing a part with no real depth of feeling or sincerity, and because 'mummer' hints at the word 'mother' it carries a double-edged thrust.

Because the passage appears in the first chapter it is clearly important in setting up key features of the novel, especially Stephen's state of mind, as we have just seen. Mulligan's part in the novel is brief but significant. As a foil to Stephen's passive and reflective moods, Mulligan is briskly indifferent, smug and self-confident, and he provides the opening section with its energy. There are many suggestions that Mulligan has a priestly role here and that Stephen is merely an acolyte at his black mass. To understand this, recall how the chapter begins, with Mulligan in superior position, blessing the landscape with the opening words of the Latin Mass ('*Introibo ad altare Dei*'), and later crossing the razor and his mirror on the shaving bowl, chalice-like, using Stephen's handkerchief as a priest's napkin. Stephen's subordination here, combined with a similar image of servitude in the second chapter together with his heavy inertia in the third, help to demonstrate how he has lost both his drive and his sense of direction.

Stephen has left home and is spending some time at the Martello tower, where in spite of the fact that *he* pays the rent, Mulligan retains the key and exploits both Stephen and the Englishman, Haines. At the end of the chapter Stephen reveals his knowledge of this by denouncing Mulligan as the 'usurper' – although the word can equally apply to Haines as a symbol of British rule in Ireland. He determines not to sleep in the tower again, adding that he will not return home either.

Thus in the first chapter we see Stephen once more preparing, in mind at least, to leave home, to set loose as a wanderer and this will be paralleled by the departure (in chapter 4) of Mr Bloom, who similarly feels he cannot return home – because of his wife's suspected adultery with Blazes Boylan, another sort of usurper.

The opening chapter sets up many such parallels between Stephen and Mr Bloom, drawing out their differences as well as their similarities. For instance, another parallel hinted at here is quite a simple, understated one, but important none the less. Notice in the last paragraph of the passage that Stephen is wearing black, as Mr Bloom will do later. Both are in mourning – Mr Bloom for his deceased friend Patrick Dignam; Stephen for his dead mother. The narrator describes Stephen's coat-sleeve as 'frayed' and 'shining', emphasising along with the dirty, crumpled handkerchief just how shabby homeless Stephen has become (we also learn after this passage that the trousers he wears are borrowed from Mulligan).

At the same time, his black apparel has symbolic overtones, for his appearance resembles that of the brooding figure of Hamlet, and you will recall that, like Shakespeare's play, *Ulysses* too opens on a castle's battlements. Stephen himself extends this Hamlet parallel in this and subsequent chapters with his 'moody brooding' and occasional outbursts of vitriolic madness against 'friends'. But why does Joyce do this? Well, I think the chief effect is to point up the fact that, like Hamlet, Stephen is effectively fatherless: he is a son in search of a father, and we are expected to see his encounter with Mr Bloom, a father in search of a son, in this light. What we see in the opening chapter of the novel is that Mulligan, as a supplier of advice as well as of second-hand trousers, is a kind of symbolic father-figure but ultimately a false one since he abuses Stephen's character and exploits his 'genius' for his own private gain. And Stephen rightly rejects him by quitting the tower.

Although to some extent the first chapter of *Ulysses* is a sequel to *A Portrait*, there is quite a gulf between the two books in terms of their styles. If you take another look at the above passage and at the whole opening chapter of *Ulysses* and compare it with *A Portrait* I think you will see how much richer the texture of Joyce's mature writing is here. In particular, notice in the final paragraph of our passage how Joyce builds up a complex interplay of theme and image, perhaps in the association between the bowl of Dublin Bay and the basin imagined at the bedside of Stephen's dying mother. If we consider, too, that the Martello tower, representing the stability which Stephen is about to relinquish, also symbolises the womb (he calls it the 'omphalos' or navel), then I think this gives a good idea of how complex Joyce's meanings can become here as well as throughout the novel as a whole.

(3) Select a second passage for discussion

Well, having examined a passage with Stephen at its centre let us move on to look at one which features Mr Bloom.

> Poor old professor Goodwin. Dreadful old case. Still he was a courteous old chap. Oldfashioned way he used to bow Molly off the platform. And the little mirror in his silk hat. The night Milly brought it into the parlour. O, look what I found in professor Goodwin's hat! All we laughed. Sex breaking out even then.
>
> He prodded a fork into the kidney and slapped it over: then fitted the teapot on the tray. Its hump bumped as he took it up. Everything on it? Bread and butter, four, sugar, spoon, her cream. Yes. He carried it upstairs, his thumb hooked in the teapot handle.

Nudging the door open with his knee he carried the tray in and set it on the chair by the bedhead.

– What a time you were, she said.

She set the brasses jingling as she raised herself briskly, an elbow on the pillow. He look calmly down on her bulk and between her large soft bubs, sloping within her nightdress like a shegoat's udder. The warmth of her couched body rose on the air, mingling with the fragrance of the tea she poured.

A strip of torn envelope peeped from under the dimpled pillow. In the act of going he stayed to straighten the bedspread.

– Who was the letter from? he asked.

Bold hand. Marion.

– O, Boylan, she said. He's bringing the programme.

– What are you singing?

– *La ci darem* with J. C. Doyle, she said, and *Love's old Sweet Song.*

Her full lips, drinking, smiled. Rather stale smell that incense leaves next day. Like foul flowerwater.

– Would you like the window open a little?

She doubled a slice of bread into her mouth, asking:

– What time is the funeral?

– Eleven, I think, he answered. I didn't see the paper.

Following the pointing of her finger he took up a leg of her soiled drawers from the bed. No? Then, a twisted grey garter looped round a stocking: rumpled, shiny sole.

– No: that book.

Other stocking. Her petticoat.

– It must have fell down, she said.

He felt here and there. *Voglio e non vorrei.* Wonder if she pronounces that right: *voglio.* Not in the bed. Must have slid down. He stooped and lifted the valance. The book, fallen, sprawled against the bulge of the orangekeyed chamberpot.

– Show here, she said. I put a mark in it. There's a word I wanted to ask you.

She swallowed a draught of tea from her cup held by nothandle and, having wiped her fingertips smartly on the blanket, began to search the text with the hairpin till she reached the word.

– Met him what? he asked.

– Here, she said. What does that mean?

He leaned downwards and read near her polished thumbnail.

– Metempsychosis?

– Yes. Who's he when he's at home?

– Metempsychosis, he said frowning. It's Greek: from the Greek. That means the transmigration of souls.

– O, rocks! she said. Tell us in plain words.

[pp. 75–7]

This passage is taken from chapter 4 (at the beginning of part II) and takes place at roughly the same time as the action of chapter 1, that is between 8 and 9 o'clock in the morning. At the Blooms' house on the north side of Dublin, Leopold Bloom prepares and serves breakfast-in-bed for his wife Molly. After brewing the tea he has gone round the corner to the pork butcher to buy some kidney and, on his return, he brings the post up to Molly, still in bed. A letter for him from their daughter Milly assures them that she is settling into her new job as a photographer's assistant in the country, and reading this he recalls her childish delight in Professor Goodwin's hat. However, there is also a mysterious letter addressed to Molly ('Mrs Marion Bloom'), in a 'bold hand'. He loads the breakfast tray for her and then carries it upstairs.

If we look for an obvious opposition or tension in the passage we will at first be disappointed but, as is continually the case in *Ulysses*, the local significance of a passage depends very much on what goes before and after it; in *Ulysses* the importance of a particular passage can only be fully understood in the context of the book as a whole. And although the tension is not yet apparent or strong, it seems to me that the passage contains a great deal which is of vital importance in terms of the book as a whole. For instance, Mr Bloom notices a strip of torn envelope under Molly's pillow. Not much in that perhaps, but the use of the single word 'peeped' makes us realise that she has hidden Boylan's letter, implying that the secret contents are concerned with more than just the programme for their forthcoming musical tour. It marks the start of one of the book's deepest tensions and will mean that Mr Bloom is forced to stay away from home for the rest of the day, preoccupied with his wife's infidelity, and returning in the early hours of the next morning when the coast is clear.

But the letter is not the only source of tension here. The choice of music which Molly indicates is also deeply ironic and the two titles will haunt Mr Bloom for the rest of the day. As you may know, the duet '*La ci darem*' is taken from Mozart's *Don Giovanni*, an opera whose chief themes are sex and seduction, and it is sung by a woman tempted into a liaison by the bold hand of the Don. And 'Love's Old Sweet Song' was a sentimental popular ditty which reflects nostalgically on a couple's early courtship. The former looks forward to Molly's assignation with Boylan; the latter looks back to her courtship with Mr Bloom – and both motifs will fill Mr Bloom's attention throughout his day. The two songs will also be counterpointed in Mr Bloom's thoughts by the chorus of jingling brasses of the marital bed (heard here for the first time) and by the repeated occurrence of the word 'metempsychosis'. The fuller importance of this word will become clear, I think, when we know more about Mr Bloom's life as a whole. Although he ardently embraces to the full the living life of Dublin, his mind is frequently drawn to thoughts of the dead, not least because he is soon to attend Dignam's funeral, but also because the anniversary of his father's suicide is approaching. Furthermore, for a variety of reasons he is possessed by memories of his dead son, Rudy, who died only eleven days after his birth, and later he will recall other deaths (such as those of Mrs Sinico and Parnell) and in this way their souls can be said to have transmigrated to the world of the living.

'Metempsychosis' is important for another reason, too. The opening chapter of Leopold Bloom's day reveals the relationship between his wife and himself, and at this moment it seems very ordinary, mundane even, and harmonious. And it seems to me that Joyce clearly intends us to see it in this way. They are ordinary people, in contrast to Stephen Dedalus, and this makes it easier for the reader to refer to and understand them. If we consider for a moment their relationship we can see that Mr Bloom, like Stephen in the previous passage, is a servant, also seen mounting stairs at the start, to bring Molly the breakfast he had conscientiously prepared for her ('Bread and butter, four, sugar, spoon, her cream. Yes.'). He offers to open the window, fetches her book, and will soon buy her another one. Later [p. 304] we see him choosing the book (*Sweets of Sin*), after buying her lotion from a chemist's, and in the evening he contemplates getting up a concert tour for her. He is dedicated to Molly and it is on these terms that we will judge *her* actions and Mr Bloom's response to her. At the same time, her request to him to explain the strange word 'metempsychosis' is a minor triumph for him and it tells us, as it tells Mr Bloom himself, that she regards him as an authority (even if he cannot explain it in 'plain words'). She acknowledges him as someone who knows and this gives him a feeling of assurance during the day, one of the slight victories over Boylan which he needs to hang on to.

Although we may describe them in the above passage as an ordinary couple, in an everyday scene, the style in which the scene is presented is not itself ordinary. The language of the passage, like its subject, works to create a cosy, homely image from the 'hump bumped' of the tray, near the beginning, through the sensual and maternal images of Molly and her abandoned underclothes, to the 'bulge of the orangekeyed chamberpot'. It is an image of domestic bliss in contrast to homeless Stephen's unhomely situation with its cold granite tower and material shortages.

The dialogue, too, seems plausible and unstrained. But the narrator's discourse describing Mr Bloom and what he does and sees is far from conventional. If you look at the language of the opening paragraph you will see how it draws attention to itself by its fragmented sentences and simple phrasing. And then in the second paragraph we are placed directly in Mr Bloom's mind's eye as he checks the contents of the tray, approves them, and then carries it upstairs. This style is typical of the early chapters of *Ulysses*, giving us external descriptions of scenes or an objective description of a character's mind and then presenting us, unwarned, with the raw unmediated thoughts themselves of the character. So in the above passage we could be forgiven for feeling confused about why a paragraph concerning a professor and his hat precedes one in which a man prods a kidney in his kitchen. The reason is, of course, that everything in the scene is observed from Mr Bloom's particular point of view, and Joyce is at pains to give us the very details of a character's thought-processes. He employed this technique in *A Portrait*, but in *Ulysses* he takes it a stage further by giving the thoughts more directly, so that Mr Bloom sounds as if he is talking to himself, in a sort of interior monologue.

Although the initial style of these first chapters of the novel may seem unconventional, I would say that when compared to later chapters it is still relatively lucid. And yet, at the same time, there are indications of the verbal experiments to come; for example, in such paradoxical expressions as 'In the act of going he stayed' and 'her cup held by nothandle', where the language (and the narrator) begins to draw attention to itself.

(4) Select a third passage for discussion

We should now move on to examine a passage from much later in the novel. Our third passage comes from chapter 12. After attending the funeral of Paddy Dignam, Mr Bloom goes about his daily business of canvassing advertisements for the *Freeman's Journal*. This takes him on an odyssey around Dublin while at the same time he is prevented from returning home in case he intrudes on Molly with Blazes Boylan. In the late afternoon he takes a light

meal in the Ormond and then waits for Martin Cunningham outside Barney Kiernan's bar. Eventually he enters and gets into a
testy exchange of words.

– Shove us over the drink, says I. Which is which?
– That's mine, says Joe, as the devil said to the dead policeman.
– And I belong to a race too, says Bloom, that is hated and persecuted. Also
now. This very moment. This very instant.
Gob, he near burnt his fingers with the butt of his old cigar.
– Robbed, says he. Plundered. Insulted. Persecuted. Taking what belongs to us
by right. At this very moment, says he, putting up his fist, sold by auction off in
Morocco like slaves or cattles.
– Are you talking about the new Jerusalem? says the Citizen.
– I'm talking about injustice, says Bloom.
– Right, says John Wyse. Stand up to it then with force like men.
That's an almanac picture for you. Mark for a soft-nosed bullet. Old lardyface
standing up to the business end of a gun. Gob, he'd adorn a sweeping brush, so
he would, if he only had a nurse's apron on him. And then he collapses all of a
sudden, twisting around all the opposite, as limp as a wet rag.
– But it's no use, says he. Force, hatred, history, all that. That's not life for men
and women, insult and hatred. And everybody knows that it's the opposite of that
that is really life.
– What? says Alf.
– Love, says Bloom. I mean the opposite of hatred. I must go now, says he to
John Wyse. Just round to the court a moment to see if Martin is there. If he comes
just say I'll be back in a second. Just a moment.
Who's hindering you? And off he pops like greased lightning.
– A new apostle to the gentiles, says the citizen. Universal love.
– Well, says John Wyse, isn't that what we're told? Love your neighbours.
– That chap? says the citizen. Beggar my neighbour is his motto. Love, Moya!
He's a nice pattern of a Romeo and Juliet.
Love loves to love love. Nurse loves the new chemist. Constable 14A loves Mary
Kelly. Gerty MacDowell loves the boy that has the bicycle. M.B. loves a fair gentel-
man. Li Chi Han lovey up kissy Cha Pu Chow. Jumbo, the elephant, loves Alice,
the elephant. Old Mr Verschoyle with the ear trumpet loves old Mrs Verschoyle
with the turnedin eye. The man in the brown macintosh loves a lady who is dead.
His Majesty the King loves Her Majesty the Queen. Mrs Norman W. Tupper loves
officer Taylor. You love a certain person. And this person loves that other person
because everybody loves somebody but God loves everybody.
– Well, Joe, says I, your very good health and song. More power, citizen.

[pp. 431–3]

The passage is related chiefly by an unnamed narrator, one of
the characters in Barney Kiernan's bar, a racist with a clearly jaun-
diced attitude to life in general and an aversion to Mr Bloom in
particular. The men in the bar have been discussing nationalism,
among other things, and they use the occasion to vent their frus-

trations and anti-Semitism on Mr Bloom. In defending the Jews, Mr Bloom seizes the opportunity to counter their hatred by his defence of love and humanity. The conflict and tension in the passage are easy to read; both have seethed from the opening of the chapter and they both intensify as the Citizen's hostility becomes more frustrated and explicit.

The principal narrator is probably a collector of bad debts, currently hired to chase up payment from a plumber by the name of Gerachty who stole tea from the Jew, Moses Herzog. And the principal character holding court in the bar-room is also anonymous, deferred to simply as 'the Citizen', a fanatical nationalist who dominates the chapter with bombast and bullying intolerance, which is invariably directed against foreigners and outsiders in general.

Mr Bloom, the quintessential outsider this day, has felt the increasing tensions both external and within him throughout the day, and they climax now in this passage. As a result, he is as ready for confrontation as his rabid antagonist, as ready to speak his mind – even though a more cautious fellow might have kept his head down. He is a handy target for their anger, a scapegoat, particularly as he insists on affirming his Jewish origins in the same breath that he asserts his Irishness, a combination which seems to be an anathema to his listeners.

They suspect that Mr Bloom is a Freemason on the make and to cap it all they suspect that he has won a packet on the big race, and that he is keeping it all to himself. Of course they never confront him on this, only hint at it. What they regard as Mr Bloom's silence and secrecy is, in fact, mirrored by their own silence and secrecy, and, importantly, these two characteristics are the basis of what we can describe as their tribalism, which necessarily excludes Mr Bloom. His 'offence' of not sharing out the 'winnings' is compounded in their eyes by the fact that he readily accepts a cigar from Joe Hynes but omits to stump up for a round of drinks. Only we, as readers, are aware of the rumours and misconceptions which victimise Mr Bloom, and the gap which opens up between what we and the characters know is the source of the acute dramatic irony in the chapter, an irony that increases the tension and the sense of futility about the events in it.

Chapter 12 is a chapter of distortions and, as the above passage reveals, even Mr Bloom's insistence on the reality of love becomes distorted and abused, which is perhaps the worst offence in the chapter because, as many readers have suggested, the theme of love is one of the central concerns of the novel.

The most dramatic distortion comes in the paragraph beginning 'Love loves to love love', which takes up and twists Mr Bloom's earlier keyword, implying that history (especially Irish and Jewish histories) has been a nightmare of force and hatred. Its rancorous tone is all one with the cynicism in the bar, though I do not think this paragraph necessarily comes from either the chief narrator of the chapter or the other men in the bar. The passage is an ironic dismissal of Mr Bloom's positive idea of 'love', distorting it through exaggerated sentimentalism. The word 'love' is repeated to such an extreme that it becomes absurd and meaningless, and yet I think this absurdity has the eventual effect of pointing up the oafishness of the men themselves.

However, in terms of Mr Bloom's character, 'love' is an extension of the many positive values which he embodies in the novel: tolerance, equanimity, compassion, charity and sensitivity among them. To see these in action we need only recall his help for the blind stripling, in chapter 8, his material assistance to Dignam's family, his service to Molly, and his offer of help and home to Stephen Dedalus. And to understand the significance of his later encounter with Stephen it is also useful to remember that for Stephen love is an enigmatic, elusive concept, a 'bitter mystery', the word known to all other men [look again at pp. 61 and 681–2]; their encounter is the meeting of the cultured all-round family man of the world (for whom love is the driving force) and a failed but promising artist.

But, to return to the passage, who is the narrator of the 'love' paragraph if, as I have claimed, it is not one of the men in the bar? We can attempt an answer to this question by looking in detail at the style of the extract as a whole. I think we have three levels of narrative here, as we do throughout the chapter as a whole. On one level are the words of the dialogue between the men in the bar, and then on a second are the words of the narrator's bilious discourse, directed against Mr Bloom (for example, the paragraph beginning 'That's an almanac picture . . . '). But the 'love' paragraph is unlike these first two levels, the range of its imagery and its comic surface suggesting that it has a different origin.

If we compare the narrative style of this extract with that of the opening chapters it creates quite a shock. In this respect it is part of a continuing movement away from the 'initial style' towards increasingly experimental modes of expression. At the same time, we also have an increase in the number and diversity of narrators whose points of view shift away from the centre of the novel's action. Here in chapter 12, for the first time in the novel, we have a chapter in which Mr Bloom's own consciousness does not appear, making his thoughts and motives uncertain, a situation which is exacerbated by the partiality and unreliability of the main narrator in it. And, of course, all of these points contribute to the reader's difficulty in the novel because they contribute to the increasing uncertainty about the reader's own position in the novel.

(5) Select a fourth passage for discussion

Our final passage comes from the final chapter of the novel and is spoken by Molly Bloom.

> . . . then they go howling for the priest and they dying and why why because theyre afraid of hell on account of their bad conscience ah yes I know them well who was the first person in the universe before there was anybody that made it all who ah that they dont know neither do I so there you are they might as well try to stop the sun from rising tomorrow the sun shines for you he said the day we were lying among the rhododendrons on Howth head in the grey tweed suit and his straw hat the day I got him to propose to me yes first I gave him the bit of seedcake out of my mouth and it was leapyear like now yes 16 years ago my God after that long kiss I near lost my breath yes he said I was a flower of the mountain yes so we are flowers all a womans body yes that was one true thing he said in his life and the sun shines for you today yes that was why I liked him because I saw he understood or felt what a woman is and I knew I could always get round him and give him all the pleasure I could leading him on till he asked me to say yes and I wouldnt answer first only looked out over the sea and the sky I was thinking of so many things he didnt know of Mulvey and Mr Stanhope and Hester and father and old captain Groves and the sailors playing all birds fly and I say stoop and washing up dishes they called it on the pier and the sentry in front of the governors house with the thing round his white helmet poor devil half roasted and the Spanish girls laughing in their shawls and their tall combs and the auctions in the morning the Greeks and the jews and the Arabs and the devil knows who else from all the ends of the Europe and Duke street and the fowl market all clucking outside Larby Sharons and the poor donkeys slipping half asleep and the vague fellows in the cloaks asleep in the shade on the steps and the big wheels of the carts of the bulls and the old castle thousands of years old yes and those handsome Moors all in white and turbans like kings asking you to sit down in their little bit of a shop and Ronda with the old windows of the posadas glancing eyes a lattice hid for her lover to kiss the iron and the wineshops half open at night and the castanets and the night we missed the boat at Algeciras the watchman going about serene with his lamp and O that awful deepdown torrent O and the sea the sea crimson sometimes like fire and the glorious sunsets and the figtrees in the Alameda gardens

yes and all the queer little streets and pink and blue and yellow houses and
rosegardens and the jessamine and geraniums and cactuses and Gibraltar as a girl
where I was a Flower of the mountain yes when I put the rose in my hair like the
Andalusian girls used or shall I wear a red yes and how he kissed me under the
Moorish wall and I thought well as well him as another and then I asked him with
my eyes to ask again yes and then he asked me would I yes to say yes my mountain
flower and first I put my arms around him yes and drew him down to me so he
could feel my breasts all perfume yes and his heart was going mad and yes I said
yes I will Yes.

[pp. 931–3]

It is now about two in the morning. Molly is lying in bed next to
her husband, though in effect the last chapter feels timeless as we
listen to the continuous stream of her thoughts flow into the surrounding dark. After reflecting on all aspects of her life, past and
future as well as present, her attention begins to fix on the memory of the picnic on Howth Head when Mr Bloom proposed to
her and they kissed and she accepted him. And then the moment
merges with the recollection of her very first kiss, with a young
officer called Mulvey, when she lived on Gibraltar.

The tension of the passage issues principally from Molly's tone
and feeling, and in particular from the sudden climax of excitement towards the end of her monologue. The turbulence at this
point, which has been growing from the beginning of the chapter,
contrasts with the peace of the night-world outside and with the
silence of her sleeping husband beside her and it indicates a
marked change in her attitude and feeling toward him, all of
which prepares for the final triumphant 'Yes', which echoes beyond the the novel into the night silence.

The passage hints, of course, at the conflicts and tension within
Molly. But at the same time she is naturally tired and her sleepy
mind interweaves past and present, Dublin and Gibraltar, and her
relationships with Bloom and Mulvey. Although her memories of
Gibraltar life and of Mr Bloom's proposal are vividly immediate,
she is never maudlin about the past: in looking backwards at key
moments of her life she never becomes sentimental, and I think
the reason is that the tensions in her thoughts give them an intrinsic vitality, as if they were recalled solely for their own sake.
Consequently her preoccupations throughout the chapter have an
intense joy about them, an ecstasy almost as fierce as the 'deep-
down torrent' she feels towards the end. So, even without her
final, beautiful 'Yes', they are an affirmation of life, and a fusion

of hope and reality. In this respect she is the antithesis of both Mr Bloom and Stephen, for whom such memories are often negative and tinged with regret.

The passage marks the grand climax to the whole novel in both its promise and its ecstasy, and converts doubt into triumph. Molly Bloom, like a great Earth mother-goddess, is a great spirit of creative energy, continually rejuvenating herself. Her mind at this point gathers up images from earlier in the chapter, and in particular those of her youth on Gibraltar together with her view of the picnic on Howth Head. As Mr Bloom had done earlier, she relives the picnic in her mind and in doing so she forms a bridge with her husband's consciousness. Her vividly detailed picture of her life on Gibraltar weaves exotic scenery and colour, with flowers – roses, jessamine, geraniums, cactuses – one of the key motifs of the chapter as a whole. As a flower herself she recalls her married name 'Bloom' (as well as her husband's pen-name: 'Henry Flower') and at the same time implies that her monologue flows like a river.

Notice, too, how, within the flow of her thoughts, her continual reiteration of the word 'yes' works like an increasing pulse, intensifying the mood of joy towards the final climax of sound and feeling. The word appears at first to act as a form of self-assurance, but then it gradually operates as a spur, moving her mind from one excited thought to the next, until it ultimately takes on a symbolic aura, echoing her reacceptance of Mr Bloom and embracing the promise of the new day which is about to dawn.

An important practical consideration about the final chapter of *Ulysses* is that it gives us Molly's intimate view of some of the same subjects which have absorbed Mr Bloom throughout the day. She offers us a mature female insight to complement Bloom's mature male insight. In particular she allows us to understand more about Milly and Rudy, and about Boylan and the afternoon affair, but above all it tells us about one of the biggest mysteries of all: Molly herself, who has been 'off-stage' and out of sight for almost the entire book (and yet constantly before our attention, through Mr Bloom's consciousness).

Molly reveals why she was attracted to Mr Bloom and why she continues to be attracted to him; namely that she could see that he 'understood or felt' what a woman is. And this confirms an idea that has been current throughout the whole novel: Mr Bloom's knack of seeing the other person's point of view, on which point he scores decisively over Boylan, the 'ignoramus'. Like her husband, Molly uses the memory of the fateful picnic at Howth as a reference point from which to view other events. Mr Bloom himself is another such reference point for her by which to compare other men, Boylan especially, and, for a variety of reasons, Mr Bloom finally emerges as the victor, at least for today.

However, throughout the final chapter Molly has catalogued all her husband's shortcomings (ultimately his endearments to her) – 'there isn't in all creation another man' [p. 917] – and perhaps this affectionate realism about Bloom makes her picture of him the more convincing, and we are thus more inclined to accept that she loves him for this reality.

On the other hand, Molly and her speech are also a medley of confusions and contradictions; the chapter will require a good many re-readings. In spite of this, readers have often looked at this final section for a possible answer to one of the big unanswered questions of the novel, namely whether or not Molly will stay with Mr Bloom. The answer is uncertain and you may like to consider the final passage on these terms. On the one hand she has earlier determined to 'give him one last chance' and, for example, serve him breakfast in bed (as he had done for her on the previous day), but she has as soon contradicted this with thoughts of the forthcoming tour with Boylan. The answer is uncertain, but perhaps the elation at the end of the chapter, an orgasmic cry of ecstasy, suggests that her real happiness lies in continued married life, lived with her husband Mr Bloom; it may not last forever – but then again what does? The strong, vivid memory of their seedcake kiss on that eventful picnic when she had decided to commit herself to him seems too deep-rooted in her consciousness for her to break up with him now, with its risk of subsequent emotional upheaval. And if this is so, then the final 'Yes' can also be regarded as an ultimate (for now, anyway) affirmation of her life with Mr Bloom, with all its imperfections.

It is possible to make other interpretations, of course, and it seems to me that uncertainty is a key feature of the novel as a whole. I use the word 'feature' rather than, say, 'problem' because I feel that is not essential to get an answer to all the questions in the novel, only to be aware of the possibility of alternative interpretations. For me at least, *Ulysses* is a comedy of human uncertainty, and ironically the final word, Molly's 'Yes', is both an acceptance of that frailty and an assurance of its inevitable renewal.

Uncertainty is, naturally, a characteristic feature of Molly's chapter too (full of confusing phrases, ambiguous expressions and pronouns, unfinished threads – she even gets her own age wrong!). And this is exacerbated by the way Joyce sets down Molly's thoughts, like a stream of consciousness, a 'stream of life' [p. 193] as Mr Bloom says, in which there is minimal punctuation and the whole is arranged into only eight paragraphs, with perhaps short silences in between them. The final paragraph begins, on page 923, with the word 'no' repeatedly attached to thoughts of Boylan and it ends, above, with the word 'Yes' finally attached to her image of Mr Bloom, a change which clearly underscores her return to her husband. At the same time the flow of Molly's language, I think, attempts to represent female language patterns, with a form and a logic of its own, as a counterbalance to the male interior monologues of Stephen Dedalus and Mr Bloom. This can be seen perhaps in the way that Molly continually uses the word 'yes' (twenty times in our extract alone), while another cardinal point of the chapter is the word 'because' or the phrase 'on account of', which act like the word 'yes' to help Molly locate herself within her conscious world, to monitor her relationship with the world by interpreting it on her own terms.

However, the apparently free style of the final chapter offers few concessions to the reader. The absence of standard punctuation makes it a little off-putting, but if it is read simply as a flow, the task is made more easy. The free style can be seen perhaps as a parallel to Molly's amoral point of view of life, but it does also suggest that the events of her day-life can be unwoven by her mind through this nocturnal consciousness. Certainly the freedom of the style, with its loose syntax and its absence of continual starts and finishes, gives an extra dimension and an extra context to the novel, freeing it from its earth-bound and finite perspectives.

The chief effect of all this is, I think, to suggest that the cycle of the day is completed by Molly and that through her being and her resolute 'Yes' it is about to begin again. The new day is approaching and, as Mr Bloom has said before, the sun shines for her.

(6) Have I achieved a sufficiently complex sense of the novel?

We have examined four passages in reasonable depth and although we have begun to appreciate some of the novel's subtle touches it will require further study before we can get an idea of the complexity of Joyce's revolutionary approach in *Ulysses*. A full discussion of this complexity is beyond the scope of the present study but we can at least take some steps towards an understanding of the scale of Joyce's achievement in the novel. So, with this in mind, I would like to look in detail at the characteristic features of the interior monologue, and at the unusual structure of the novel. In addition, I think we should look closely at some of the special ways in which Joyce creates his meaning in the novel and, related to this, we should touch on the nature of ambiguity and uncertainty in the text.

II Aspects of the Novel

The following extract is taken from chapter 8 of *Ulysses*:

He threw down among them a crumpled paper ball. Elijah thirty two feet per second is com. Not a bit. The ball bobbled unheeded on the wake of swells, floated under by the bridge piers. Not such damn fools. Also the day I threw that stale cake out of the Erin's King picked it up in the wake fifty yards astern. Live by their wits. They wheeled, flapping.

> *The hungry famished gull*
> *Flaps o'er the waters dull.*

That is how poets write, the similar sounds. But then Shakespeare has no rhymes: blank verse. The flow of the language it is. The thoughts. Solemn.

> *Hamlet, I am thy father's spirit*
> *Doomed for a certain time to walk the earth.*

– Two apples a penny! Two for a penny!

His gaze passed over the glazed apples serried on her stand. Australians they must be this time of year. Shiny peels: polishes them up with a rag or a handkerchief.

Wait. Those poor birds.

He halted again and bought from the old apple woman two Banbury cakes for a penny and broke the brittle paste and threw its fragments down into the Liffey. See that? The gulls swooped silently two, then all, from their heights, pouncing on prey. Gone. Every morsel.

Aware of their greed and cunning he shook the powdery crumb from his hands. They never expected that. Manna. Live on fishy flesh they have to, all sea birds, gulls, seagoose. Swans from Anna Liffey swim down here sometimes to preen themselves. No accounting for tastes. Wonder what kind is swanmeat. Robison Crusoe had to live on them.

They wheeled, flapping weakly. I'm not going to throw any more. Penny quite enough. Lot of thanks I get. Not even a caw. They spread foot and mouth disease too. If you cram a turkey, say, on chestnut meal it tastes like that. Eat pig like pig. But then why is it that saltwater fish are not salty? How is that?

His eyes sought answer from the river and saw a rowboat rock at anchor on the treacly swells lazily its plastered board.

Kino's
11/-
Trousers.

Good idea that. Wonder if he pays rent to the corporation. How can you own water really? It's always flowing in a stream, never the same, which in the stream of life we trace. Because life is a stream. All kind of places are good for ads. That quack doctor for the clap used to be stuck up in all the greenhouses. Never see it now. Strictly confidential. Dr Hy Franks. Didn't cost him a red like Maginni the dancing master self advertisement. Got fellows to stick them up or stick them up himself for that matter on the q.t. running in to loosen a button. Fly by night. Just the place too. POST NO BILLS. POST IIO PILLS. Some chap with a dose burning him.

[pp. 192–3]

I chose this passage not because there is anything odd or exceptional about it but really for the opposite reason, that it seems so typical of Mr Bloom's thought processes, of the form and substance of his interior monologue, and it is this which I would like to look at first in this section.

On a first reading the passage appears to be not much about anything really, just some idle thoughts not geared into any particular direction. But closer inspection of this (and every other passage) will reveal not only the nature of its internal operations but also how important it is in helping to build up the complete text.

To put the passage briefly into context first, Mr Bloom is walking by the river ('Anna Liffey') in the centre of Dublin, having conducted his business in the *Freeman*'s news office in the previous chapter. A young man presses a throwaway handbill onto him announcing the imminent arrival of Elijah, the prophet who predicts the arrival of the Messiah, and this triggers off at least two thematic elements. One of these is that 'throwaway' is another oblique reference to the winner of the afternoon's Gold Cup horserace – which Mr Bloom has already and inadvertently predicted to Bantam Lyons [p. 106]; and the other is that Mr Bloom will also, in chapter 15, visualise himself facetiously as the Messiah, a bringer of 'light to the gentiles'. Later, when he feeds the Banbury cake to the hungry gulls, he ironically uses the word 'manna', perhaps indicating that he already pictures himself in this way. It may also give us a clue as to the significance of his meeting with Stephen Dedalus, to whom Mr Bloom brings the 'word', the mysterious 'word known to all men', on which Stephen himself has been meditating [p. 61].

The hungry gulls bring to Mr Bloom's mind a fragment of verse, a rhyming couplet, and this leads him on to a quotation from *Hamlet*, another feature which connects him with Stephen Dedalus, as we have seen already. The play is important not only as the basis for Stephen's Shakespearean theorising (referred to in chapter 1 and expounded in chapter 9) but also because it refers to his search for a consummate father, in the absence of his own real father. By quoting the line 'I am thy father's spirit' Mr Bloom adds further weight to the suggestion that he symbolises a sort of spiritual/artistic father-figure, while Stephen represents for him a surrogate son in the wake of Mr Bloom's real son, Rudy. And Mr Bloom's reference here to foot and mouth disease (in the middle of the extract) is yet a further connection with Stephen since the latter has just delivered Mr Deasy's sententious letter on this topic to the editor of the *Freeman* (in the previous chapter).

That Mr Bloom should misquote Shakespeare's verse ('earth', instead of 'night') seems entirely typical of him. He is not, like Stephen, an intellectual or an academic, as his definition of poetry also indicates. His formal education is a simple, basic one and in effect he is really a self-educated man. His reading is unstructured but encyclopaedic (see the catalogue of his library on pp. 832–3) and it tends to be recalled very imperfectly and in fragments – like the formula for the acceleration of falling bodies referred to at the start of the extract: 'thirty two feet per second'. Much tends to be speculative or just hearsay, such as the mistaken idea that gulls spread foot and mouth disease and that Robinson Crusoe lived off swans, which is also untrue. But what actually focuses Mr Bloom's thoughts quite dramatically both here and on his wanderings is the subject of advertising in all its manifestations. For him the subject is not just an idle amusement, but a highly specialised and persuasive art-form.

As a canvasser of advertisements, this comes as no surprise of course but he takes it to such extraordinary lengths that he often appears to be searching for the perfect advertisement. He admires Kino's acumen in using a rowing boat on which to mount his advertising boards free of charge, and he notes its prime position too, like that of Dr Franks' ad 'stuck up in all the greenhouses' (when you realise that in Dublin slang a 'greenhouse' is a gentlemen's urinal, it seems a perfect place to advertise the services of a VD doctor!).

Thus, what seems at first to be a completely chaotic random mess of ideas is actually a chaotic random mess of ideas which is structured through Mr Bloom's consciousness, one thought triggering off the next, even though on the surface it may seem incomprehensible. In theory, at least, every passage in the novel can be explored in this way and the connections made, the silences and gaps filled. But of course this needs research and close reading and this is exactly what Joyce demands of his reader. For instance, you could ask what the point is about 'Erin's King', mentioned in the opening paragraph. Naturally, Mr Bloom does not explain, even though the reader would sometimes like him to. But ask yourself 'why not?' Well, the simple reason is that, because he already understands the point, there is no need to explain it to himself (in case you are wondering what Mr Bloom is referring to, have a closer look at pp. 81 and 495 where he recalls a rough boat-trip with his daughter, Milly, round Dublin Bay to the Kish lighthouse). So his reflections, references, images and so on often seem obscure because what we see are his direct unmediated thoughts, in the raw, and as well as the contents themselves we are given a strikingly intimate psychological insight into the reality of Mr Bloom's thought processes, and in particular an insight into the manner in which he links his fragments together. What we see is in fact the highly developed form of Joyce's technique of 'indirect free style' which we met in *A Portrait*, but now offering the reader a much closer and more accurate representation of the thoughts themselves, without the intervening narrator.

What we have, then, in this technique of showing a character's inner thoughts or interior monologue is a sort of stream, a 'stream of consciousness' as it is called, and if we look again at the final paragraph in the above extract we see that Mr Bloom himself is alluding to this very idea when he compares life itself to a stream – always flowing – 'which in the stream of life we trace'. And so Joyce's technique of the stream of consciousness here is just such a trace, attempting to tap the very process of conscious thought; and Mr Bloom himself confirms this idea when he reflects, in the second paragraph, that poetry is the 'flow of the language'.

In *Ulysses* Joyce gives us the detailed interior monologue of Bloom and Stephen, yet, as we have seen above, Molly's monologue in its relentless flow is the one which most closely resembles a stream, like the river 'Anna Liffey' herself, mentioned in the extract. And there are other interior monologues in the novel – those of Tom Kernan in chapter 10 [pp. 307–10], and Gerty MacDowell in chapter 13, and of the unnamed narrators in chapters 14 and 16. Each has its own distinctive features, reflecting the mind patterns of its originator. But in general terms the interior monologue consists of an accretion of words, unfinished sentences and phrases, sensations, perceptions, memories and images, together with fragments of song, verse, speech, scientific formulae, and advertising copy. Where Stephen's interior monologue clearly reveals his erudition, in its sophisticated sequence of academic allusions, that of Mr Bloom tends to be wandering, unfocused, piling up perceptions on top of each other in an agglomeration of material. Generally, the contents of Mr Bloom's monologue arise more often from his immediate environment. It is characteristically speculative and most often it focuses on people and objects. Its component units tend to be shorter than Stephen's. At the same time, a recurring feature of Mr Bloom's interior monologue is a tendency to reverse the usual syntax of a sentence; for example, from the above passage,

> Australians, they must be this time of year
> Live on fishy flesh they have to . . .
> Good idea that.

Both Bloom's and Stephen's thoughts are composed of fragments, or condensed sentences, often with words omitted. On the other hand, if you have another look at Molly Bloom's interior monologue, you can see that it is much freer, like an uninterrupted stream, giving the impression of a long unbroken rhythm, but one fed from an emotional fountain whose point of reference is invariably the inner self.

Because Molly Bloom is pictured only in bed and at night (apart from a glimpse of her arm in chapter 10) her monologue has few references to the immediate local setting. Mr Bloom's, on the other hand, continually refers to the local setting. His passive but receptive mind makes him open to a vast amount of external stimuli, in minute particulars too. He is observed continually making connections between these detailed outside events and his internal responses to them. We see his world through his own eyes, of course, but it is a world which is constructed from within by Mr Bloom himself rather than imposed from outside.

By using Mr Bloom's (and Stephen's and Molly's) stream of consciousness to reveal the world, Joyce also opens up the possibilities of alternative meanings, and in a manner which has a very naturalistic appearance. Indeed, as you may have already discovered, the minute details of the novel frequently become interesting in themselves since they often adopt a life of their own (as chapter 15 especially shows). However, because of the way in which Joyce's characters notice and respond to the minutiae of their lives, such details invariably take on symbolic importance too. This means that, as well as revealing the inside of, say, Mr Bloom's mind, they also reveal him in his environment as a citizen, revealing other characters within a corporate Dublin and, in so far as they take on symbolic and mythic functions, these details further open up the context to embrace Irish and European cultures and history. This may sound over-ambitious, perhaps, but in the next stage of our analysis I hope to show how Joyce broadens the scope of his novel from a simple day-in-the-life story to one which takes on wider epic and cosmic dimensions.

I mentioned above that in Mr Bloom's stream of consciousness Joyce gives the appearance of a random mess of ideas. However, in order to create this appearance he takes great care in its composition. Joyce once told a friend that he had spent all day working hard on some aspect of the book, and when asked if he had therefore written a lot replied that he had written two sentences! He explained that he had spent the whole day in just getting the words in the right order. He took immense pains over the order or form of his work, not only in *Ulysses* but in all of his writing. So what might appear at first to be formless often has a very intricate pattern underlying its surface, and this applies not only on the level of the individual words and sentences but, as we might expect, in terms of the novel as a whole. I think we should now explore the form of the novel and to do so we can start at the very beginning by considering the title of the novel itself.

Ulysses. You must have wondered about it. Why is the book named after a figure from ancient Greek mythology who never appears in it? There are several references to the Greeks: Buck Mulligan calls Stephen an 'ancient Greek', Mr Deasy tells Stephen that Helen was to blame for the fall of Troy, while Mr Bloom (who writes Greek *e*'s in his letters to Martha Clifford) is described by Mulligan as 'Greeker than the Greeks'. There are hints, but the real significance of the title lies submerged beneath the surface of the novel in the structure that Joyce used in composing his story. Ever since, as a schoolboy, he had first read Charles Lamb's *The Adventures of Ulysses* (an adaptation of Homer's *The Odyssey*), Joyce had been charmed by the adventures of the Greek hero who was condemned to roam the Mediterranean for ten years after the fall of Troy. So in writing his novel Joyce set out to parallel the ancient travels of Ulysses with the single-day roamings around Dublin of a Jewish advertising canvasser. In being forced to stay away from home (by his business commitments as well as a fear of bursting in on Molly and Boylan), Mr Bloom is compelled to undergo his own odyssey on the streets of Dublin.

To help make the analogy to Homer more relevant, Joyce closely tied his own hero's adventures into those of Ulysses by making each chapter of *Ulysses* correspond to an episode from *The Odyssey*. Therefore, in chapter 4, Molly's repose in bed is intended to parallel the island of the nymph Calypso who detained Ulysses on his return from Troy. Later, Mr Bloom's visit to the Glasnevin cemetery parallels Ulysses' visit to the underworld of Hades, and the episode in the newspaper offices (chapter 7) corresponds with the journey to King Aeolus who gave Ulysses a bag of winds to aid his return home (however, you may recall that a suspicious crew opened the bag prematurely and they were blown back to Aeolus – as Mr Bloom is rebuffed by the newspaper editor over the renewal terms of the Keyes advertisement).

As you read chapter 7, however, you are very unlikely to be aware of the parallels with Homer's episode. Yet the hints are there. Have another look at the chapter and note the countless references to the wind, for instance. In a similar way the parallels between Joyce's chapter 5 and Homer's equivalent episode are equally obscure. In chapter 5 Joyce had in mind Ulysses' adventure in the Land of the Lotus Eaters where his crew became intoxicated by eating the lotus and desired only to remain there, forgetful of their homeland; in Joyce's chapter, Mr Bloom is assailed by a vast range of drugs, seductive lotions and languorous fragrances – from the cigarettes of its opening paragraph, through aromatic brews and flowers, to the lemon soap at the chemist's and dreams of a relaxing bath.

Table 1

Chapter	Joyce's episode	Homer's episode
I		
1 Telemachus	Stephen, haunted by the death of his mother, determines to quit the Martello tower for good.	Athene urges Telemachus to be independent of his mother and to search for his father Ulysses.
2 Nestor	Stephen at school receives pay and advice from Mr Deasy.	Telemachus seeks news of his father from King Nestor.
3 Proteus	Stephen struggles with his artistic failure; he feels there may be an important rendezvous this evening.	Telemachus visits Menelaus who relates his struggle with Proteus, who revealed that Ulysses was on the island of Calypso.
II		
4 Calypso	Eccles Street. Bloom serves breakfast to Molly who conceals Boylan's letter.	Ulysses is imprisoned by Calypso, the 'Concealer', on her island.
5 Lotus Eaters	Bloom tours central Dublin, receives flower and buys lemon soap from chemist.	Ulysses diverted to land of the Lotus Eaters where his crew forget their homeland.
6 Hades	Bloom attends Dignam's funeral and thinks of death and the women he has known.	Ulysses visits Hades and meets the spirits of his dead mother and other women he has known.
7 Aeolus	Bloom tries to renew Keyes' ad but returns to news office and is spurned by editor.	Aeolus gives Ulysses a bag of winds but near home his crew open it and are blown back.
8 Lestrygonians	Bloom is surrounded by images of food and eating.	The king of the Lestrygonians, a cannibal, eats some of the crew before Ulysses escapes.
9 Scylla and Charybdis	The Library: Bloom passes between Stephen Dedalus and his friends in dispute.	Ulysses takes a course between the cliff of the monster, Scylla, and the whirlpool, Charybdis.
10 The Wandering Rocks	Nineteen short sections which overlap in time and are at first difficult to follow.	This represents a route among treacherous rocks, rejected by Ulysses.
11 Sirens	Ormond Bar. Bloom writes a reply to Martha while the men are charmed by music.	Ulysses resists the deadly lure of the Sirens' song by binding himself to the ship's mast.
12 Cyclops	Barney Kiernan's bar. Bloom is assailed by the insults of the bigoted Citizen.	Ulysses and his crew are trapped by one-eyed Polyphemus but escape by blinding him.

Table 1 – continued

13	Nausicaa	Bloom observes Gerty and her friends playing ball. She is attracted to the dark stranger.	Washed ashore, Ulysses is woken by Princess Nausicaa who befriends him.
14	Oxen of the Sun	Maternity hospital. Students endorse fornication and contraception. A sudden thunderclap is heard and chaos follows.	Ulysses' crew slaughter the sacred oxen for a feast and are killed by a thunderbolt from Zeus.
15	Circe	In Bella Cohen's brothel surrealistic episodes suggest bestiality and the collapse of rationality.	The witch Circe drugs the crew and turns them to swine. Ulysses, protected by a magic herb, forces her to release them.
	III		
16	Eumaeus	Bloom takes Stephen to cabman's shelter for drinks. Bloom sees him as possible singing partner for Molly.	Disguised, Ulysses returns, stopping at Euemaeus' hut until he meets his son and they plot the slaughter of the suitors.
17	Ithaca	Back home Bloom and Stephen drink cocoa. Bloom comes to terms with Boylan and Molly.	Ulysses in disguise slaughters Penelope's suitors after a test of strength.
18	Penelope	Molly, woken by Bloom, recalls her early life and loves.	Penelope is woken by news of the slaughter but does not at first recognise Ulysses.

Not surprisingly, when *Ulysses* was first published its readers did not detect these parallels and were puzzled by the title of the novel. Joyce decided to make the Homeric structure and the correspondences more explicit by drawing up a schema of his novel showing the titles of Homer's episodes linked into his own. Table 1, adapted from Joyce's schema, attempts to summarise the parallels (the Homeric titles are the ones which Joyce used for the composition of his chapters and although he removed them from the published text they are still used to refer to individual episodes).

Table 1 gives a reasonable idea of the structure of the novel, but you can see that some of the similarities are a little oblique or tangential; for instance, the connections between Homer's 'Sirens' or 'Cyclops' episodes and Joyce's equivalent chapters are quite tenuous. In each correspondence Joyce rarely makes a one-to-one parallel between what Ulysses and Bloom each do, and it would be very difficult (and banal) to make twentieth- century Dublin correspond that closely to the world of Homer's hero. Instead, he distils the quintessence of Homer and translates this through metaphor and analogy to the Dublin of 1904. Thus in chapter 11, 'Sirens', Mr Bloom resists the seductive allure of the two barmaids, Lydia Douce and Mina Kennedy, who have charmed the other men in the Ormond Bar, by binding himself metaphorically to the task of composing a reply to Martha Clifford. Joyce's 'Cyclops' opens with the narrator complaining that he almost had his eye knocked out by a sweep; yet the principal equivalent of Homer's Polyphemus is the one-eyed prejudice of the Citizen (and of his cronies in the bar) who eventually hurls a biscuit tin at Mr Bloom (instead of a huge rock, as in Homer).

For this device of symbolic correspondences Joyce used the term 'expressive form' and it is fascinating to trace the correspondences. But it is important to understand their significance too. Joyce did not use them simply as a conceit, and clearly they have an important structural role in the novel, helping to hold together what would otherwise appear to be a very loose sequence of episodes.

In addition to Mr Bloom's journey around Dublin there are many other odysseys within the novel, not least of which is Stephen's since he leaves the Martello tower in the morning vowing never to return. Like Telemachus' search, Stephen's odyssey, too, can be considered symbolically as the quest for the 'father'. Blazes Boylan and Lenehan also have their own odysseys around Dublin, though their exact routes are uncertain, and the seaman in chapter 17 who calls himself 'Murphy' has been away from his wife and home for seven years . . . or so he claims [p. 719]. Even Mr Bloom's lemon soap, bought in Sweny's chemist in 'Lotus Eaters' (but not paid for), undergoes a sort of odyssey, a *saponiad*, as Bloom switches it from one pocket to another around his body.

There is, however, a more important point to the correspondences and this is the moral effect which Joyce creates from them. This becomes the more important if you notice that, as in *A Portrait*, Joyce nowhere makes any direct moral comment in the whole of the novel, with one exception: the title itself, *Ulysses*. To imagine the effect of this, try to imagine the novel without this title, or with some other title: *A Day in the Life of Leopold Bloom* perhaps, or *Mr Bloom Takes a Walk, The Adventures of an Ad-man*. In this way, the title *Ulysses* sets up expectations for the reader here, just as the word 'Artist' did in *A Portrait*.

At the same time, I think that the moral effect in *Ulysses* comes less from the similarities with Homer than from the differences, perhaps the most obvious one being the contrast in the characters of Molly and Penelope. In *The Odyssey* a celibate Penelope spends the ten years of Ulysses' absence in fending off suitors, maintaining her fidelity by the ruse of weaving and unweaving a shroud. In Joyce's novel, however, Molly, who has not had full sexual intercourse with her husband since the death of their son, Rudy (a period of 10 years, 5 months, 18 days), not only yields to Boylan's charms but appears to solicit them. And, of course, the contrast with Homer's idealised heroine depicts her in a very poor moral light, at least until she weaves her web-like monologue in the final chapter.

Another important contrast exists between the respective central characters of the two works. Mr Bloom's return home is as low key as that of Homer's Ulysses was, but the significant difference lies in the ways in which the two heroes deal with their rivals on return. After a test of strength Ulysses ruthlessly slaughters the suitors in spite of the fact that they had been completely unsuccessful in seducing Penelope. On the other hand, when Mr Bloom enters the marital bed, a bed which still bears the marks of Molly's afternoon love-making, he reflects on Boylan's infamy, and where we might have expected him to take some form of revenge he simply does not. Instead he gradually comes to terms with the outrage by rationalising it, putting it into perspective, and distancing himself from it:

> With what antagonistic sentiments were his subsequent reflections affected?
> Envy, jealousy, abnegation, equanimity.
>
> [p. 864]

He does not forgive Boylan, and he will certainly not forget the outrage, but by understanding the nature of adultery and by placing it in the contexts of far worse offences (such as robbery, blackmail, arson, manslaughter and murder) he puts it into an objective perspective and triumphs. His drowsing mind allows him to dissipate the impact of the betrayal as well as of his profound sadness by the cool realisation that physical retribution would be equally unethical. It casts him in a strong moral light. And from what Molly says (he has apparently demanded breakfast in bed the next day) it seems, too, that he is about to impose a new form of home rule.

By using the myth of Ulysses Joyce perhaps also imbues his vision of modernity with a pessimistic reality, by comparing present-day realities with the mythic past. The idealised heroism of Homer's tale undoubtedly satirises the mediocrity and relativism of the present. But it can also work the other way because the novel has the effect of demythologising the past, by suggesting that Ulysses was still an ordinary man, a man like Mr Bloom, at once a father, a son, a husband, a lover, a companion of men: making a hero of the everyman-Bloom, and an everyman of the hero-Ulysses. Certainly the parallels with Homer's work help to give the novel its epic dimensions in spite of its single-day scenario, stressing the human continuity between the ancient and the modern. And in this way, Joyce also suggests that the problems which face Mr Bloom are timeless.

The structural correspondence with *The Odyssey*, then, provided Joyce with a ready-made form by which to order his material. But, as I have suggested above, this form is effectively submerged beneath the surface, and so to hold his vast text together Joyce had to turn to other features. The singleness of the day and the unity of the place, Dublin, help of course to tie the novel together, but they are not by themselves sufficient and we must look, I believe, to character for the key to the novel's unity.

Joyce limits his main characters to the two strongly developed individuals at the centre and the chief organising principle of the text arises from the relationship which develops between them, beginning even before they meet. The recurring motifs within their respective interior monologues support this principle, while at the same giving the novel its moral impetus. Examples of these motifs include, for Mr Bloom: the deaths of his father and son, Molly's infidelity, a dream from the previous night, various advertising slogans, two important dinner parties, the day of the Howth picnic and his engagement, the letters from Milly and Martha, Plumtrees Potted Meat (without which no home is complete), and the importance of love. For Stephen, recurring motifs include: the death of his mother, unfulfilled artistic ambition, intellectual preoccupations with Hamlet and Aristotle, literature, Catholicism, and the mystery of love.

And yet struggling against this principle of unity (and in constant tension with it) is an equally strong impulse toward plurality and decentring. Perhaps the clearest manifestation of this is the diversity of styles and points-of-view which Joyce adopts. Why does Joyce do this? Well, one reason is that he loved the challenge of imitating the styles of other writers. Another is that his parodies contribute much humour to the novel. And a third is that the range of styles helps establish an ironic texture, one style set off against another, and this enables Joyce to control the reader's responses, which is an especially important point given that Joyce refuses to intrude his own moral view directly on the events or people of the novel.

The sudden switches in style also have a very disruptive effect on the reader's attention, as you must have discovered, and these, together with the gaps and silences in the text, act to break down the conventional relationship between the reader and the novel. The text has a habit of turning away from the reader, of evading, and I think this puts the onus on the reader to look for information to fill the gaps and ultimately to create meaning.

These gaps, or silences, are an important feature of Joyce's style and I would like to study their effects further. I will use as our starting point a short extract from 'Ithaca' (chapter 17), which occurs as Mr Bloom is preparing for bed, and he contemplates the possible wording of an advertisement which someone might devise following his disappearance:

What public advertisement would divulge the occultation of the departed?

£5 reward lost, stolen or strayed from his residence 7 Eccles Street, missing gent about 40, answering to the name of Bloom, Leopold (Poldy), height 5ft 9½ inches, full build, olive complexion, may have since grown a beard, when last seen was wearing a black suit. Above sum will be paid for information leading to his discovery.

[pp. 857–8]

One of the things that may strike us about the style of this section in the novel, more so than any other, is the way it tries to reduce everything to an impersonal, objective description. It appears to be stripped of any artifice (though really it isn't) and to be, above all, truthful and candid. It is, of course, exaggeratedly materialistic. For instance, it tries to reduce Mr Bloom to a few lines of external description (age, nickname, height and appearance), a description which reveals in particular the shortcomings of the conventional materialistic approach of traditional novelists. But by extension it also suggests the limitations of the novel as a whole since the novel, too, is a sort of 'public advertisement' of Mr Bloom. In fact the 'Ithaca' chapter reveals how such a materialistic approach absurdly fails to come close to its subject since it can only deal in facts and measurable quantities. Its silences are almost as equally important as its statements and are certainly more voluminous; the more it says the more we are aware of what is left to say. In an important sense, the silences of 'Ithaca' are a paradigm for those of the novel as a whole.

The silences of 'Ithaca' begin with the anonymity of the two voices in the chapter, one asking the questions and the other responding, and like the headlines of 'Aeolus' they both appear suspended and disembodied in space. It is almost as if in the quiet of the night the idea of personality itself has dissolved, leaving us with a 'Noman' amid the cold of interstellar space. Perversely, the style often presents us with little of what we feel we want to know, while at other times it is effusive on the seemingly irrelevant (such as the source of the water in Mr Bloom's taps). It leaves us with the unmistakable impression of a style striving to obscure.

'Ithaca' gives us lots of facts, of course, a bit like an encyclopaedia. But it does not evaluate. And even if it did we could not be sure whose values they were. Joyce leads us to the conclusion that, inevitably, a finite work of literature cannot embrace the infinity of information which is available, and then also to the realisation of the uncertainty and ambiguity which this gap implies. He draws attention to the uncertainties implicit in a text but, not content with this, his cryptic style sometimes resembles a riddle in which the reader is drawn in like a detective (Joyce actually boasted to a friend that he had put in so many enigmas and puzzles that it would 'keep the professors busy for centuries').

So 'Ithaca' is a chapter with its tongue in its cheek, feigning to reveal while all the time aware of what is unsaid or concealed. And, as the final chapters of what we could call the 'male sphere' of the novel are reached, any expectations of a denouement or a revelation are ultimately disappointed – while at the same time the novel gives the impression of closure. But this vast novel has no denouement; it has no conventional untangling of a plot or a resolution of a moral problem. For one thing, it has no conventional plot and its interests are not single but multifaceted (with multiple points of view and consciousnesses) without making any

one of them privileged over the rest. Equally, Joyce does not re-
solve any of its moral problems and, still less does he even hint at
his own point of view about them.

To understand Joyce's attitude here more clearly I think we
should consider particular examples from the novel, ranging from
materialistic points of fact to complex ethical issues. For instance,
in 'Hades' who is the mysterious man near Paddy Dignam's
funeral? The man is anonymous but through a misunderstanding
he becomes known as M'Intosh (and his name is later printed
as such in the *Telegraph* – see p. 751). What is the meaning of
the epigram 'U.P.' on Mr Breen's card [p. 199], and what is the
message which Mr Bloom scratches in the sand at the end of
'Nausicaa' [p. 498]? Why does Stephen's hand hurt in 'Circe'
[p. 687]? And, importantly, what will Mr Bloom and Molly – and
Stephen – do 'tomorrow', 17th June 1904?

Joyce's text raises such questions and encourages us to find our
answers by making connections across the fragments scattered
through the different streams of consciousness (though if you happen to discover the definitive answers to any of these questions
you should drop me a line immediately). Other examples, however, entail more ethical considerations. For example, how should
we react towards Molly's adultery? It seems immoral and our first
reaction might be to condemn her out of hand, but the issue is
not simple; she herself feels troubled at first, then mitigates herself on the grounds that she was obeying a natural impulse. Mr
Bloom, too, feels he has neglected her for over ten years. So our
response is unlikely to be clear cut. In addition, Molly's adultery
raises other themes besides those of marriage and fidelity, such as
the nature of the family and then, further afield, of filial responsibility, which concern Stephen as well as Mr Bloom.

On the broader ethical scale, the novel invites discussion about
the power and influence of both the Catholic Church and the
British Empire on the lives of Dubliners. And Joyce draws attention also to questions about the relationship between self and
community, especially in terms of political and racial indulgence.
As we read *Ulysses* we cannot help but feel that the novel springs
from a strong ethical conviction (as well as from comic roguery),
but if you look for a clear philosophy from Joyce all you will get is
a shrug of the shoulders and a sardonic smile.

Some readers have suggested that the whole novel is ironic,
chiefly because of the stylistic parodies, and that it mocks heroic

values by depicting a modern world of relativity and uncertainty. Others have claimed the very opposite, that the ironies of *Ulysses* do not mock its values but in fact help to present a set of alternative and positive values. One such view is that the novel condemns pride and commends charity, typified by Mr Bloom's rejection of violence as a solution to the outrage of his marriage. Another is that the novel represents the triumph of love, in its widest possible meaning. This view places importance on the role of Stephen too, in his quest for the 'word known to all men', and what his mother describes in *A Portrait* as the need to learn what the heart feels.

But whether or not we accept these views might depend on how we interpret the convergence of Mr Bloom and Stephen, a convergence which the text presents in symbolic terms, not least in the 'Ithaca' chapter:

> What two temperaments did they individually represent?
> The scientific. The artistic.
>
> [p. 798]

However, it would, of course, be crass to see the novel simplistically in terms of these two temperaments alone. Mr Bloom is described in a wide range of aspects: he has a touch of the artist, he is the new womanly-man, a cultured allroundman, a Wandering Jew, a Gentile, the new Messiah for Ireland, a Freemason, a cod, a mackerel, and a dark horse, a swaddler, a wolf in sheep's clothing, 'Mr Knowall', Everyman and . . . 'Noman', a range of ideas which only hints at his complex personality. And yet the convergence of the two temperaments of, let us say, the artist and scientist, is the major organising principle of the novel and it is anticipated from the very beginning of the novel (and even before it in the dreams which Stephen and Mr Bloom each have on the previous night, prefiguring their encounter). They are united symbolically at various points in the novel, at its emotional climax in 'Circe' and finally and most significantly (I believe) in Molly's thoughts at the end.

Reading and re-reading *Ulysses* is very much a question of living with the silences and uncertainties which help to generate its tensions and its vital energy. Joyce gives no definitive moral answers: he presents the possibility of meaning rather than a final revelation, and the 'truths' of the novel are only versions of the truth. And in 'Penelope' Molly subsumes and rewrites the previous seventeen chapters, now expressed through her own realities. We have seen something of how the obscurities and silences affect these versions of the truth and there is, in addition, a restlessness about the text, issuing from its ironies and its doubts, and from the absence of a central unifying voice in the novel. It is this restlessness which defers certainty and denies any final reductive interpretation. Yet, for me, what emerges from the text is Joyce's brilliant vision of a 'jocoserious' comedy of folly and endeavour, a vision of what it is to be human, in which the whole text forms a single, ultimately timeless epiphany, forever returning its reader to begin yet again this stately plump book of Bloomsday.

5

Finnegans Wake: 'the purest kidooleyoon'

I Constructing an overall analysis

Whenever someone asks me if I have read *Finnegans Wake* I find that just as I am about to reply, I have to stop myself and ask them what they mean by the word 'read'. That's what *Finnegans Wake* does. The book makes you question in a radical way what you mean by words like 'read', 'novel', 'plot', 'character', 'themes'. It makes you hesitate about itself because as soon as you begin to say something about it, to embrace it, it disables your words with its own, its vast deconstructing cosmos swallowing up all attempts to encapsulate it finitely.

With each of his new works Joyce revolutionised the form of the novel, but the leap forward to *Finnegans Wake* (published in 1939) was by far the greatest. It was a startling new departure for Joyce as well as for the form of the novel – if novel is what it is. Many people have questioned even this, while others have described it as a nightmare, the nightmare of history. However, I prefer to think of this brilliant, enigmatic, frustrating, sexy and indeterminate book of books as a work of magic and fun, a 'joyicity' of delight, and 'the purest kidooleyoon'. And the best way to start to read it is on these terms.

So what *can* we say about this magnificent 'funferall' (a typical Joyce play on the words 'funeral' and 'fun-for-all')? Well, given the limitations of space here we cannot do much more than introduce its enormous universe, but I think we can begin by attempting to describe its pattern.

(1) After reading the novel, think about the story and what kind of pattern you can see in the text

(In the following description a paragraph is allocated to each of the four Books of *Finnegans Wake*, while chapter numbers are shown in brackets. Page numbers refer to the Faber edition – though almost all current editions follow the same pagination.)

(1) The opening pages of the book (which are a continuation of its closing page) are a sort of overture spanning the fall, wake and rise again of Finnegan, before the scene dissolves into a description of the topography and history of Dublin and its environs, the whole landscape of which is pervaded by Finnegan's gargantuan presence. He is revived by the mention of whiskey but as he stirs he is pacified by the mourners at his wake. Meanwhile, the mysterious H C Earwicker arrives and displaces him, setting up his pub with his wife and children, a daughter and two sons. (2) Questions and rumours proliferate about how HCE got his name and about his possible misdemeanour in the Phoenix Park, and these increase after he meets a tramp (the Cad) in the park who tells his wife. The gossip grows and climaxes eventually in 'The Ballad of Persse O'Reilly'. (3) The rumours and gossip become distorted into a mist which clouds the truth about HCE. After he is imprisoned a series of gossiping characters present different versions of him and his identity gradually merges with those of other figures, including his enemies. (4) He is submerged and buried beneath Lough Neagh but as his trial by the Four Masters begins for whatever he did in the park, he transforms into a fox and mysteriously disappears. (5) His wife Anna Livia Plurabelle (ALP) enters, singing a great litany of praise to her husband, a 'mamafesta', and presents a twisted fragment of a letter to the court for analysis but, though it promises much, it remains a mysterious collection of baffling signs and interminable possibilities probably written by one of her twin sons, Shem the Penman. (6) Her other son, Shaun the Post, materialises onto the scene, and as a Professor Jones he sets up a judicial self-examination in the apostolic form of twelve quiz questions. He relates the parable of 'The Mookse and the Gripes', another manifestation of the conflicting twins, this time hinting at the political dealings of the English Pope Adrian. (7) Shem is presented by his brother Shaun as 'Pain the Shamman', scandalous fraudster and debaucher, a dirty-minded composer of pornography gone prematurely blind and half mad. (8) The beautiful song of ALP the river flows quietly by, between two washerwomen on opposing banks of the Liffey. They feverishly exchange a chorus of gossip about ALP and HCE's sin, washing their dirty linen in the chittering water. HCE's desire for

his own daughter Isabel is glossed over through the alluvial gifts distributed by ALP and then night softly falls.

(1) While HCE dreams, his children enjoy a tea party in front of the pub. Shem and Shaun now metamorphose as Glugg and Chuff with their sister Issy and her twenty-eight rainbow girl-friends, and they play games and the riddle of 'colours'. With a sudden thunderous roar HCE calls in his children and all the girls run away home. (2) The children set about doing their homework in a quest for knowledge across a range of subjects. The twins' comments are presented as marginal notes in a textbook, Shem's in the left margin (as Dolph) and Shaun's in the right (as Kev). (3) Meanwhile, inside the pub a great boisterous party is going on and we overhear noisy anecdotes interspersed with fragments of a radio broadcast and glimpses of the television double act of Butt and Taff. We hear the story of the Norwegian captain who orders a suit and is cursed by the tailor when he complains of the poor fit. And then there is the tale of how Buckley shot the Russian general in the act of relieving himself. Closing time comes and HCE swigs up the dregs from his customers' glasses, then col-lapses in a drunken stupor. (4) He slumps on his four-poster bed. The posts transform into the Four Masters or judges, 'Mamalujo', while before them HCE fantasises the Arthurian legend of Tristan and Isolde in which as King Mark he is cuckolded by his young son, Tristan.

(1) HCE falls into a deep dream evoking Shaun's domination of Shem, the former presenting his jealousy as a lecture on space and time, the fable of 'The Ondt and the Gracehoper'. The letter reap-pears, carried by Shaun who attempts to read and deliver it, but he mutates into a barrel and rolls away bumping downstream. (2) Coming to rest on a bank, Shaun gives a moralising sermon to Issy then flirts with her twenty-eight followers. His sermon urges a conventional morality, prudish and repressive, and he chastises Shem as a writer of obscene material. Issy dreams of her phantom lover. (3) Shaun/Yawn now appears as a spectral personification of HCE, the sleeping giant in the park. Sleeping on the dump he is interrogated by the Four Masters. Gradually the voice of HCE is heard defending himself as a respectable citizen who loves his wife and is innocent of any crime. ALP supports her husband and extols his fidelity as well as his frailty. (4) The scene reorientates to the four-poster in HCE's bedroom where the passionate love-making of HCE and ALP is suddenly interrupted by a cry from

Shem/Jerry. After comforting him they continue, silhouetted against the window as dawn approaches.

At about six o'clock in the morning, with daylight increasing, objects in the room and the landscape begin to clarify. The family start to wake. Night-death is over. Breakfast is mentioned and ALP's letter reappears in an extended version in the form of a monologue. Her husband rises, reborn, the same anew, and their identities fuse with those of their children, the past working through the present to the future. It is Easter, another rising, another resurrection, hope swelling like a river in flood. ALP is again the river, spilling over the estuary and passing into the sea, ready to return once more to the mountains/HCE and begin again the cycle of recirculation, to take us back to the first page of the book.

What does this description tell us about the book? Well, it reveals just how difficult it is to do justice to this magnificent work in trying to reduce its encyclopaedic proportions to a few lines. It reveals, too, how the notions of 'plot' and 'character' are really quite irrelevant to it. Yet, I hope also that it gives some idea of the magic of the work, particularly in terms of its evanescent reality, its instabilities and transformations, and its restlessness (with people turning into rivers or mountains, or even into other people). I have also tried to reveal something of the tensions in the text, which arise from its recurrent conflicts and from the book's persistent moral tone and themes. What we need to do now, I think, is get closer to the text by examining a passage in detail and trying to see how Joyce creates these special effects.

(2) Select a short passage from the novel and try to build upon the ideas you have established so far

I have decided to take a look at a passage from Book I, chapter 5, in which a mysterious letter is unearthed and described, with hints that it might bear on the question of what HCE did in the park.

The bird in the case was Belinda of the Dorans, a more than quinquegintarian (Terziis prize with Serni medal, Cheepalizzy's Hane Exposition) and what she was scratching at the hour of klokking twelve looked for all this zogzag world like a goodishsized sheet of letterpaper originating by transhipt from Boston (Mass.) of the last of the first to Dear whom it proceded to mention Maggy well & allathome's health well only the hate turned the mild on *the van* Houtens and the general's elections with a *lovely* face of some born gentleman with a beautiful present of wedding cakes for dear thankyou Chriesty and with grand funferall of poor Father Michael don't forget unto life's & Muggy well how are you Maggy & hopes soon to hear well & must now close it with fondest to the twoinns with four crosskisses for holy paul holey corner holipoli whollyisland pee ess from (locust may eat all but this sign shall they never) affectionate largelooking tache of tch. The stain, and that a teastain (the overcautelousness of the masterbilker here, as usual, signing the page away), marked it off on the spout of the moment as a genuine relique of ancient Irish pleasant pottery of that lydialike languishing class known as a hurry-me-o'er-the-hazy.

Why then how?

Well, almost any photoist worth his chemicots will tip anyone asking him the teaser that if a negative of a horse happens to melt enough while drying, well, what you do get is, well, a positively grotesquely distorted macromass of all sorts of horsehappy values and masses of meltwhile horse. Tip. Well, this freely is what must have occurred to our missive (there's a sod of a turb for you! please wisp off the grass!) unfilthed from the boucher by the sagacity of a lookmelittle likemelong hen. Heated residence in the heart of the orangeflavoured mudmound had partly obliterated the negative to start with, causing some features palpably nearer your pecker to be swollen up most grossly while the farther back we manage to wiggle the more we need the loan of a lens to see as much as the hen saw. Tip.

[pp. 111–12]

What we have here is the first of a series of letters in *Finnegans Wake*, and yet they may in fact all be aspects of the same letter. Here, after a hen named Belinda scratches up the letter from a midden heap, it is examined and some of its contents are revealed, though the details are far from clear. In addition, we are given some information about materialistic aspects of it: it is on a large sheet of paper, from Boston perhaps, and it has a stain, a teastain on the bottom of it. The final paragraph begins a section in which the letter undergoes a thorough analysis, including an examination of that stain. The first technical analysis is by a chemist but it seems that close inspection leads to two results: a statement of the obvious which was already known at the outset, and/or a distortion of the subject through the process of inspection.

I chose this passage because it seems to me that the difficulties of reading and understanding the letter are similar to those of the book as a whole. For this reason, I think that the most obvious tension in this passage arises between the reader and the text itself. The reader feels that the text is telling us something but it distorts what it reveals and at the same time omits a lot of information which would make the passage's meaning clearer.

Joyce hints at a conventional letter by providing lots of the formal aspects of letter-writing, such as 'Dear', 'Allathome's health well', 'don't forget', 'hopes to hear', 'must close now'. But it looks like a parody of a real letter and, as always with *Finnegans Wake*, the text seems partly to be turned away from the reader. So just as begin to get a grip on the text it wriggles out by withholding the information that the reader thinks he or she needs. Which can be a frustrating experience – if you try to read it like a normal text.

So we have the impression of a letter, a 'missive', but without the reality of it explicitly before us to examine we cannot fix the contents. It is a bit like listening to someone skim-reading a letter aloud – *they* know what it is about but they do not make it explicit. The text is obscured by the context, by what is going on around it. But this presupposes that we should be trying to reconstitute a letter by looking for the missing bits, rather than looking at what is actually there – and this is a common mistake in reading the *Wake*. Let us see, then, what we have got.

The hen which unearths the letter is over fifty years old ('quinquegintarian') and 'Cheepalizzy' implies both the setting of the book (Chapelizod, a district of Dublin near Phoenix Park) as well as ALP's daughter, Issy or Isabel. In 'Cheepalizzy's Hane Exposition' there is a further reference to the all-important hen and its exposing of the letter, but also a suggestion of ALP's husband, Earwicker, in the initial letters CHE which are one of a multitude of transpositions and contortions of his own signature throughout the book: 'HCE'. This suggests that it is ALP herself who has discovered the letter, at midnight ('klokking twelve', with hints here too of clucking). She may even have written it herself since it refers to 'Maggy', Isabel's mysterious double in the book, and Isabel is often a representation of ALP as a young girl, her early dreams and aspirations. So for this reason the letter may be a memory of ALP's youth and her marriage to HCE, as well as a projection of his fall/death, his 'funferall', his funeral and his joyful wake. By sending 'fondest' to the 'twoinns' it also recalls her twin sons, Shem and Shaun.

The letter appears to have been written on the 31st of January – if that is what the 'last of the first' refers to. The stain is apparently important, but ambiguous; it is a teastain but van Houtens was a brand of chocolate, which may have spilled over onto the page when the heat turned the milk ('hate turned the mild'). In any case, the word 'stain' imparts a clear moral tone to the letter and, together with the point that it was unearthed from a midden heap ('mudmound'), it implies a guilty secret, another reference to Earwicker's uncertain crime in the park ('masterbilker' combines masterbuilder and cunning).

The teastain also connects with the reference to 'Boston (Mass.)' by way of the famous teaparty and this hints at a political dimension to the letter, since it hints at the theme of independence, particularly Irish independence, a contemporary problem during the years when Joyce was composing *Finnegans Wake*. The reference to 'whollyisland' supports this interpretation, suggesting as it does both 'holy Ireland' and 'the whole island' (the 'four crosskisses' can represent the Four Masters, the early chroniclers of Irish history, who recur throughout the book, often in the form of HCE's four-poster bed). For this reason, the letter as a work of literature is marked off as a 'genuine relique of ancient Irish pleasant pottery', or peasant poetry.

The final paragraph reveals that in addition to the fact that we have to guess at the contents, part of the letter is physically missing or distorted due to decomposition while it was in the mudmound. Add to this the point that the process of analysis (by any 'photoist worth his chemicots') also distorts the object under scrutiny and our difficulties are compounded. Furthermore, in order to take an objective view of its nature (its 'horsehappy values') we must take a step back from the text – with the risk that as we do so, 'the more we need the loan of a lens to see as much as the hen saw'.

Joyce mocks the process of analysis by exaggerating its methods and for the rest of the chapter (I.5) the letter undergoes a series of further and equally futile tests. Described by a professor figure, these tests go into great detail around the edges of the document while failing to focus on the letter itself.

Like any passage from *Finnegan Wake*, it is difficult to do justice to the letter without reference to the rest of the book, a fact which is more true of *Finnegans Wake* than of any other book. Clearly a full treatment of the *Wake* is beyond our scope here, but I hope that I have shown how the letter above carries metaphorical as well as archetypal significance, representing the 'text' as a whole, not just of the *Wake* itself but of any text, and of the difficulties of saying anything meaningful about it. Elsewhere in Book I, chapter

5, the narrator makes this point more explicit as he examines the envelope, the lines, the handwriting and the punctuation, 'under the pudendascope'. But perhaps the best advice is not to concentrate 'solely on the literal sense or even the psychological sense' [p. 109].

This is just one of the hundreds of letters in the *Wake*. Or perhaps, as I have suggested, they are all different aspects of the one described on page 111. The most substantial one is that in the final chapter, beginning on page 615 'Dear. And we go on to Dirtdump. Reverend. May we add majesty?' It is a beautiful piece and in addition it bears on the letter we have been considering, from I.5. It refers to many of the same points as ours (Boston, Maggy's tea, HCE's scandal, the funeral/wake), though the mood is different, subdued, gentle, anticlimactic. In a passage of great lyrical beauty, ALP quietly reflects on her early lovers and, as the river Liffey, she is about to return to the sea, to regenerate herself, and she takes her leave of dear dirty Dublin at the estuary ('Dirtdump'; which also recalls our 'mudmound') to return to her source, as the book will return after the final page to the first page. And the word 'Reverend' (river end? ever end? reve rend?) in that letter echoes the opening word of the whole book, 'riverrun', a point which implies that once more the letter stands for the whole text of this, and any other book.

I would like to close this discussion of the passage by looking briefly at the language which Joyce uses and which is probably the most stunning feature of the book. Although it appears at first to be impossibly puzzling, Joyce tends to use standard sentence construction throughout, slotting in non-standard vocabulary, as Lewis Carroll does in his poem 'Jabberwocky'. So his sentences should not cause us any problems. But the words are a different matter, and in *Finnegans Wake* Joyce really draws attention to the word as a basic unit of meaning, and questions this idea. His favourite devices are inventing new words and using elaborate puns. Compound words meld two or more existing words such as, from the above passage, 'funferall' (funeral + fun for all), 'masterbilker', 'twoinns', 'chemicots'. And puns in the passage include 'hate' (heat), 'whollyisland', 'pottery', 'pleasant'. Some are simple sound-puns, others more contrived, while others again are multilingual: 'terzis' contains the Italian for 'third' and the Turkish for 'tailor', 'Hane' is Danish for 'cock', 'zog means 'young' in Albanian, 'tache' is 'stain' in French while 'tch' suggests the

Chinese for 'tea' ('tcha') and 'boucher' hints at French words for 'mouth', 'block' and 'butcher'.

These word games, plus puzzles and riddles, are good fun and they help to intensify the themes of the book. By using polydimensional puns and compounds Joyce also creates a multilayered text, with meanings working on different levels at the same time, though we have to work hard if we want to grasp anything like all of them. And yet, if you have read any of Joyce's other works, you will know that he likes to play with these words for their own sake too, simply for the joy of their 'soundsense'.

(3) Have I achieved a sufficiently complex sense of the novel?

The answer to this question would have to be a resounding negative. Although we have seen something of how Joyce creates the possibility of meaning in a passage, I think that in order to understand the complexities of the book we need to look more closely at the problem which I raised at the beginning of our discussion, that the book seems to be able to thwart all attempts to define it. In other words we should try to understand how it is that Joyce makes us hesitate when we try to answer even quite elementary questions about his final work.

II Aspects of the novel

I imagine that in this section you may be expecting me to explain what *Finnegans Wake* is all about. Well, to be honest, I cannot tell you what it is all about and in fact the book seems to try continually to frustrate attempts at discovering what it is 'all about'. When someone tries to answer this question about a more conventional novel they might traditionally begin by separating the content from the method and next go on to outline the plot, describe its characters, and explore its themes, and then itemise the methods the author uses, perhaps finishing off with a neat comment about how effective or typical it is. In this way a reader would, of course, draw a line around the work and tie it up like a dead animal. *Finnegans Wake* continually resists this type of approach, evades any lines drawn around it, and makes the reader hesitate in the face of its indeterminacy. These things lead us to the realisation that at least for *Finnegans Wake* the question 'what is it about?' is essentially irrelevant.

This does not mean, however, that we must remain silent, and the book has generated an enormous amount of speculation and discussion. We simply have to take a different approach.

The approach which has been tried most often is to see the book as exploring the world of a dream, and this is a very practical way of accounting for the lack of clarity in it while still saying that it is about something. In a dream, characters and plot seem to break down, experience and memory are restructured and distorted in a new, less easily described way, but one in which the method and the content merge as one substance, so the way of the dream is actually at the same time the substance of the dream. In other words if you were to try to analyse one of your dreams you could not justifiably distinguish the plot of it from the way in which your mind had presented it because the one is inextricably a part of the other.

Dreams and death are two of the book's recurring preoccupations and both of these are consistent with the breakdown of continuous identity which it presents. But it is not, I think, a search for identity; the novel itself does not strive to find the identity of the dreamer. Nevertheless, because the book seems to be concerned with names, relationships and internal revelation, it also gives the impression of being concerned with character, while at the same time continually denying it.

It is almost as if the dreamer were constantly denying his own identity, effacing his 'self', while the reader is induced to go in the opposite direction and search for the origins of the dream and the dreamer, as if there were another book behind *Finnegans Wake* which we had to recover or rewrite in our own form. Instead, I think that we should accept the book on its account.

There are hints of what we normally call character or identity, and they emerge in fragments, often in a cipher or disguise, continually repeated but continually altering. So it often seems we are immersed in a riddle of merging and dissolving personalities. Lots of references cluster around the initials 'HCE' and 'ALP' as human presences, and they appear in many different guises on almost every page; for example, H. C. Earwicker [p. 33], Here Comes Everybody, Haveth Childers Everywhere, Howth Castle and Environs, H_2CE_3, Helpless Corpses Enactment. There are other clusters associated with HCE such as Tim Finnegan the builder or hod-carrier, Adam, Noah, King Mark, Humpty Dumpty, King Roderick, Finn MacCool, King Hamlet and Claudius, Dublin itself, and Ireland.

All these and many others merge and HCE takes on their identities. As they do so, HCE gathers archetypal significance: he is the father, cuckold, faller-sinner, riser-mountain. ALP appears as Anna Livia Plurabelle [for example, on pp. 215, 297, 553], HCE's wife, and she is associated with Eve, Noah's wife, Mary as the Madonna, the river Liffey, and the archetypal mother. Their children are manifested in different ways too. Shem is Cain, Ham, the Gripes, the Gracehoper, a tree, and Joyce himself, while Shaun is Abel, Japhet, the Mookse, the Ondt, a stone and Joyce's brother, Stanislaus. Isabel figures as the rainbow, nuvoletta (a small cloud), Ophelia, Mary as the Virgin, and Joyce's daughter.

But characters also merge and speak through one another. They have multiple personalities and work on different levels too. HCE is often an abstraction rather than a real person, while Shem and Shaun can represent primal conflicts or tensions within HCE, and ALP might suggest the mediation or the transcendence of them.

Character traits emerge and are observed within a pattern of repetition and the same is true of 'themes'. And like characters, themes have no explicit realisation or resolution. They appear in *Finnegans Wake* less as formulated features of a discussion than as the preoccupations of a consciousness which is in permanent flux.

We can discuss 'themes' by starting with the setting. The reference points of the book are initially the city of Dublin and surrounding areas ('Howth Castle and Environs'), but they are eventually broadened into the universe of the sleeping/dead consciousness, and the most recurrent theme is the members of HCE's family. The family and its internal relationships become the dominant focus of the book, and in particular the trinity of father–mother–child and the mystery of creation. The thunderous hundred-letter words which rumble throughout the text are constant reminders both of God and of the big bang of Creation, while the words themselves are the analogues of the mystery of human creativity, all of which are framed within the cyclical form of the book [examples of these hundred-letter words can be found on pp. 3 and 90; but see below too].

Joyce intensifies the theme of the family by his pervasive use of the Tristan myth from Arthurian legend in which Tristan, who is sent to escort his father's bride, Isolde, falls in love with her and they elope. By a process of transmogrification Joyce draws out the full incestuous and Oedipal connotations of this myth, identifying the key features with HCE, Shem/Shaun and Isolde. And, by extension, the Oedipal sin invokes that of Adam against the Father-Creator, which in turn emphasises the book's theme of the Fall.

One consequence of this is the pervasive presence of sin and guilt which stalks the consciousness of the book. On a simple level there is HCE's sin in the park, reiterated throughout Book I, which may not be an actual sin, so much as one merely dreamt of; it appears to involve indecent exposure ('supreme piece of cheeks' [p. 564]) or masturbation ('Mastabatoom' [p. 6]), while there are frequent suggestions of HCE's incestuous desire for his daughter Issy ('ensectuous from his nature' [p. 29]). As always in the *Wake*, particulars become extended and generalised into archetypes, and HCE's guilt and fall are transmuted into a general haunting sense of guilt, expressed most often as Original Sin.

But his Original Sin is not simply that of Adam and Eve (and by extension, mankind), but also of God himself in the act of creation (and perhaps the stammering hundred-letter words are an admission of his guilt). But for HCE his deep consciousness of guilt appears as a motive for the re-enactment of man's perpetual cycle of fall and resurrection, the guilt which initiates history and keeps the cycle in motion.

Joyce underlines this theme of human fallibility through the countless versions in the book of St Augustine's aphorism '*O felix culpa*' (O happy sin); for example, this is rendered punningly on page 23 as 'O foenix culprit'. It expresses an acceptance of human frailty and the inevitability of sin, incontrovertible facts of human nature, which are equally entailed in the concepts of redemption and resurrection (symbolised in *Finnegans Wake* by the river's eternal cycle of regeneration).

These are, of course, central elements in the book's themes of sleep/death and waking/rebirth, a point reflected in the pun in the title: 'fin' or 'end', again and wake (and Joyce himself explained to a friend that the book was a 'resurrection myth'). The book is probably set at Easter time [see pp. 85 and 347], and thus it refers in part to the Christian symbolism of rebirth, but Joyce interfused the *Wake* with references and winks at many other spiritual texts as disparate as the Koran and the Egyptian Book of the

Dead, most of which have reincarnation or metempsychosis as a central motif. The theme of resurrection is directly alluded to in the multifarious references to Dublin's Phoenix Park (the scene of HCE's transgression, or '*foenix culpa*'), and in the river and the rainbow, while almost every page has a reference to the egg. And by returning the reader from the final to the first page, Joyce also involves *us* in the process of renewal, each time creating the novel afresh, the 'seim anew' [p. 215, and throughout].

In addition to the spiritual books, Joyce utilised his vast reading in a wide variety of literatures to construct the encyclopaedic 'chaosmos' of his final work. Besides his old favourites, including Ibsen, Blake, Homer, the Bible, Shakespeare, the Catholic Mass, and the music hall, he enlisted an enormous and diverse amount of other literary material from many cultures: the Arabian Nights, the Book of Kells, Rabelais, Dante, Goethe, Wagner, Icelandic *Eddas*, the *Encyclopaedia Britannica*, Virgil, Rimbaud, Wyndham Lewis, Lewis Carroll, Edward Lear, Le Fanu, Swift, Hegel, Freud, St Patrick, St Kevin, the Mabinogian, Tolstoy, Malory, Moore, Mangan, and Milton, Aquinas and Anonymous. Joyce recycles his own books, too, for the new text [see pp. 114, 179 and 186] and the *Wake* frequently refers even to itself [see pp. 143, 276 and 375].

This does not mean that you would have to read all or any of these sources. In any case, to do so you would have to be what the *Wake* describes as 'that ideal reader suffering from an ideal insomnia' [p. 120]. No, the book can and should be enjoyed simply on its own account.

However, given this phenomenal weight of allusive material, Joyce needed to imbue his cosmos with some sense of architectural structure – and we have seen already how much in his other novels he was concerned with the idea of order and form. To the new reader of the book, *Finnegans Wake* perhaps presents an intimidating world of chaos, and yet underpinning it is Joyce's acute sense of order and it is this which gives the work its 'plot'. In reality 'form' here carries out the role that 'story' would perform in a conventional novel. In fact I would say that through the book's form it tends to proliferate its themes rather than simply to narrate them.

We should therefore take a closer look at the sort of form which Joyce uses in the book. Just as he made use of other writers for his allusions, he imported others sources for his ideas on form too. In this respect he looked particularly to two Italian philosophers, Vico and Bruno. Giambattista Vico regarded history as a cyclical process in which the progress of mankind moved through three principal ages, which he called (i) the divine, (ii) the heroic and (iii) the human. After the third age was completed, there followed a *ricorso*, a transitional phase during which there was flux and confusion before the cycle began anew. In *Finnegans Wake* Joyce matched each of the four books to Vico's 3 + 1 structure, the cyclical form again emphasising the *Wake*'s key theme of regeneration. Not only the four books of the *Wake* but the sequence of chapters within each book follow this 3 + 1 pattern and some readers have even traced it in the structure of individual sentences.

The other major influence on the form is the heretic Giordano Bruno of Nola, who had for long been one of Joyce's favourite thinkers [see the reference to him in *A Portrait*, on p. 271]. Joyce admired him chiefly as a free-thinker but in *Finnegans Wake* he made use of Bruno's doctrine of the 'coincidence of opposites'. Briefly, this can be stated as: every power in nature must evolve an opposite in order to realise itself, and from this antithesis a new synthesis is generated [see p. 92, line 8 of the book for Joyce's version of this theory].

In the *Wake* this doctrine is manifested on one level in the continual juxtaposition of opposing entities: Shem and Shaun, the Mookse and the Gripes, Ondt/Gracehoper, time/space, father/son, all of which are invariably conflicting aspects of the same individual. On another level it is expressed through the innumerable oxymoronic phrases such as 'sinister dexterity' and 'the seim anew'. There are hundreds of references to Bruno the Nolan, though typically, Joyce celticises him by deliberately confusing him with the Dublin booksellers Browne and Nolan for comic effect [for instance, see pp. 38, 159 and 211].

In the absence of a conventional plot what we have, then, are two organising principles, one pressing forward (Vico's) and the other (Bruno's) an impulse towards arrest and, like Shem and Shaun, the two are in constant tension. The two principles are also reflected in the way the language of the book operates. On the one hand, language is of course linear in the sense that we normally read words in sequence, and with a sense of beginning and ending. But on the other, Joyce endeavours to give his language the quality of simultaneity, and he attempts this through the use of two key language games: puns and compound words. Puns are important in the *Wake* for a number of reasons; for example, they permit a multi-plicity of meanings and they have an undoubted comic effect which supports Joyce's satire. Furthermore, in terms of a dreamscape they also symbolise the uncertainty and evasiveness of the unconscious. Here are some dairy examples:

> Burrus and Caseous . . . in the dairy days of buy and buy   [p. 161]
> [a pun on two characters in Shakespeare's *Julius Caesar*]

and

> as different as York from Leeds   [p. 576]
> [or chalk from cheese!]

As the book itself says, 'every word will be bound over to carry three score and ten toptypsical readings' [p. 20]. The result is that every word can be interpreted on a variety of levels – literal, symbolic, allegorical, moral.

Joyce's pun words have a spiralling effect on the mind of the reader; it is a vocabulary of mutations in which meanings cluster together and flourish throughout the text. Compound words (the fusing together of two or more words) have a similar effect, but seem capable of even more complex compressions than puns: for example, funferall, tallowscope, collideorscape, Finnagain, Romunculus Remus, abcedminded, Vatandcan.

In *Finnegans Wake* the basic unit of construction for Joyce is not the word but the syllable, and in terms of its musicality as much as its meaning. For this reason he stressed that to enjoy the book the reader did not need to explicate it, but simply to read it aloud, and make 'soundsense' [p. 121]. The best examples of this are the hundred-letter words which occur throughout. Perhaps they represent God's voice or thunder, a door slamming, HCE farting . . . as well as countless other possible things too. And yet they seem to me to be great fun just on account of their sounds:

> Pappappapparrassannuaragheallachnatullaghmonganmacmacmacwhack-
> falltherdebblenonthedubblandaddydoodled
>
> [p. 332]

Other examples can be found on pages 3, 23, 44, 90, 113, 257, 314, 414 and 424 (though the last one has a hundred and one letters!).

Joyce explained that the book was an attempt to render the unconscious sleeping mind, and that this could not be achieved with a regular plot and standard grammar and vocabulary. In that case, his language can be regarded as closely analogous to the dream realm of human existence, as a sort of night language. The book thus works as a self-contained universe of its own, a 'chaosmos' governed by its own laws, without necessary reference to the wideawake realm, and this is another reason for seeing the book as a thing in itself rather than as a conventional novel to be expli- cated by reference to something outside of it. In other words, *Finnegans Wake* is really about itself – it is not about something else, but it is that something.

In creating its own system or grammar, *Finnegans Wake* also cre- ates its own ideal reader (if not that one 'suffering from an ideal insomnia'). It seems to me that it tries (successfully) to break down our expectations and to deconstruct our ideas about what consti- tutes a novel. It continually refers to itself:

> Can you rede . . . its world? . . .   [p. 18]
> the learning betrayed at almost every line's end . . .   [p. 120]
> the lingerous longerous book of the dark . . .   [p. 251]
> like another telmastory repeating yourself . . .   [p. 397]

and it creates its ideal reader by continually giving explicit advice too:

> Now, patience; and remember patience is the great thing . . .   [p. 108]
> So now, I'll ask you, let ye create no scenes in my poor primmafore's wake.
> [p. 453]
> His producers are they not his consumers?   [p. 497]

However, while Joyce acknowledges and anticipates his readers I think it is important not to fall into the fallacy of searching for Joyce's intention in *Finnegans Wake*. Many readers spend their time scouring Joyce's notebooks in what seems to me a pointless search for what he set out to achieve. It seems fairly obvious that what he set out to achieve was the *Wake* itself. There is nothing else, nor do we need anything else other than what we already bring to it and find in it, to complete its 'onesidemissing' [p. 119], which is the reader's contribution. It seems to me, too, that this great book can absorb any interpretation or literary theory, which is based on its words, words 'suggestive, too, of so very much more and capable of being stretched, filled out' [p. 109]. And the more the reader puts into it, the greater will be the 'funferall' from its rich, exhilarating polyphony.

6

Writing an essay on Joyce

Writing an essay on a novel or on a writer is an important part of enjoying an author's work because it allows you to reflect and write down your response to what you have read. It gives you the chance to get down your own interpretation of the text(s) you have studied. If you are writing an essay as an exam answer or as an assignment for a course, then it is important to approach the task of essay-writing in an organised manner, to get your ideas down in a systematic format.

One of the commonest failings in essay-writing is for someone to depend heavily on being 'inspired' – as if they were writing a work of art and had to sit around waiting for their own personal muse to fill them with some mystical impulse (this is often used as a handy, but weak, excuse for putting off writing the essay). Instead, it is better to approach essay-writing in a more objective frame of mind: as something to be approached in a highly methodical way, with solid organisation, a clear sense of what is required by a question and a thorough knowledge of the text on which it is based, together with a clear understanding of your own attitude towards the issues involved in the text (and if you do have a personal muse it is likely to be impressed by this sort of organisation and to come swiftly to your assistance to fill out the framework).

Many students write essays with little or no idea of what general features an examiner or teacher expects from an essay and, so, before we look at a suggested method of essay-writing, I think it will be useful to consider briefly what is expected. This will give us some useful ideas about the method we should adopt.

In general terms, students are expected to show a detailed knowledge of a text, to answer the question as it is set and to write a coherent essay in a lucid style. More particularly, they are expected to build up their answer in clear and logical steps, making close reference to the text in question and commenting or evaluating features as the question requires. Your teacher or examiner will be rigorous in marking your essay, so you, too, will need to be rigorous in your approach to writing it. With these points clear in our mind let us now examine the stages in writing a good essay.

1   The essay question

In an examination you will probably have a choice of essay questions and, naturally, it is important to make a wise choice. Take great care at this stage because, given the time constraints of an exam, once you have chosen the question, there is no going back. It is crucial to choose a question which you know a lot about – I know this sounds a bit obvious but students often make a mistake at this stage and discover too late how little they actually do know about a particular aspect of a text or an author.

It is important, too, to pay close attention to the words of the question – the key is to decide at the outset what exactly the question is after. In this context, essay questions usually fall into two types:

(a) *Those which ask the student directly to discuss an essay topic; for example,*

> *Discuss the role which family relationships play in Stephen Dedalus's development in 'A Portrait'.*

(b) *Those which give a quotation and ask the student to evaluate the statement in the light of a text or texts; for example,*

> *Joyce said of 'Dubliners' that 'the odour of ashpits and old weeds and offal hangs round my stories'. How far do you think 'Dubliners' presents a picture of depressing lives lived in squalid conditions?*

Examiners are also fond of using key words in their questions, which students frequently misunderstand, perhaps through a hasty reading of the question or just blind panic. Such words include 'characterisation' (which refers to the *methods* that an author uses rather than merely calling for a 'character-study') and 'comment' (which implies that you should evaluate or criticise aspects of a text). Additionally, I have yet to come across a question which

says 'Write all you know about "X"', but some students still write
essays as if the question was a personal invitation to write a brief
encyclopaedia about 'X'. Make sure you understand the question
before you proceed to the next stage.

2 Making a plan

Very few people seem to want to write a plan for an essay. Which is
odd, given the difficulties of writing a good essay and the fact that
your examiner or teacher will expect to find a logical development
of ideas, building them up towards a reasonable conclusion. A
plan is a highly important strategy because it will help you to structure all the ideas which you will mobilise in the writing of your
essay. It will impose a pattern on them.

But a plan is important, too, in helping you explore an essay
question, revealing whether you really do know enough to answer
it or not. And a third reason for making a plan is that it will act as
an aid to your memory, so that when you reach page 3 of your
essay you do not suddenly forget what you were going to say next.

My suggestion for creating a plan is first of all to write down
some random notes about the title as ideas begin to come to mind
– in brief – so you can see the sort of material you might use. And,
then, having done that, shift these notes into a logical order, using
brief headings to summarise the main parts of the essay – four or
five sections should suffice for the average length of essay. An
example, using one of the above essay-titles, will help:

> *Discuss the role which family relationships play in Stephen Dedalus's development in
> 'A Portrait'.*

Looking carefully at the question, I would say that this essay
divides naturally into two aspects, thinking about Stephen's *relationships* with members of his family, and thinking about how
these affect his *development*. Next, I would jot down some ideas as
they came to mind, and then place them under these two headings:

Relationships with mother, father, brothers and sisters, Uncle
Charles and Dante (auntie) Riordan (though she
may not be a blood relative). Influence on

	Stephen. Conflicts? Plus Stephen's awareness of past family through his father's memories.
Development	Stephen as an artist.
	Stephen as a person.
	Achieves independence.
	Decline of family fortune. Rise of his own fortunes.

I would next think about key moments in the text, which could give me more detailed information about Stephen's relationship with family members and his level of development at different times, and I would do this in the same way that I have chosen passages for this study. So I might pick the Christmas dinner episode in chapter 1, Stephen's trip to Cork with his father in chapter 2, and then a passage from chapter 4 to explore the differences between the life of Stephen and that of his brothers and sisters; from chapter 5, I would consider two passages, one from the beginning and one from near the end, from Stephen's discussion with Cranly, and I would use these to examine conflicts between Stephen and his parents regarding his intellectual and artistic aspirations.

All of these would help me in formulating a plan for the essay and I would then write the plan down, something like this:

Part 1	Stephen's early life – relationships with mother and father – respect for them – life as a child.
Part 2	the influence of Uncle Charles and Dante Riordan – freedom and terror.
Part 3	Stephen and his brothers and sisters – his opportunities.
Part 4	Stephen as a young adult: conflicts with mother and father – the conflict of art and religion – loyalty to self versus duty to family.
Conclusion	Stephen's independence as an artist weighed against his growth as a person.

This seems to me a good working structure with which to tackle the question, using the notes which it has generated to fill in the details in the next stage.

3   Writing the essay

I have spent a lot of time on the planning stage of the essay but I feel this is justified because I am convinced that this is the key stage in the whole process. And if you consider what we have done in the planning stage, you will see that, in effect, most of the hard work of preparation has already been done. All that remains is the relatively simple task of writing up the notes, while taking care at all points to keep strictly to the question as asked.

Some people might say that you should start your essay by coming up with a really eye-catching sentence. While this is all right if you have plenty of time at home to work one out, I do not think you should spend valuable time in an exam trying to do this.

However, your initial sentence should engage directly with the question, and this will help keep the rest of the essay focused on the relevant topics. Work through each of the sections of your plan, drawing on material from the author's text to support the observations that you make. Using quotations direct from the text can be very useful to strengthen your arguments, but it is not usually necessary to do this, or to learn a long list of quotations for an exam. Equally, you should avoid quoting long passages – an essay is a test of your ability to respond sensitively and critically to a text, not a test of memory. In any case, it is usually sufficient simply to refer closely to episodes in a text rather than to quote passages verbatim.

Another thing to avoid is falling into the trap of merely telling the story (unless, of course, a question specifically asks you to do this – and such a question would, typically, ask you to *outline, describe,* or *give an account of* an episode from the text). But such questions are rare and are usually set as preliminary exercises rather than as examination tasks.

You should, by keeping conscientiously to the subject of the essay-question, score marks with each sentence that you write. In this respect, avoid resorting to waffle – a reader can easily spot this – and also avoid repeating material because, obviously, no one can expect to score the same marks twice for the same material. Express yourself clearly and coherently in a style which is not self-consciously elaborate, because this can distract your reader away from the content of your essay. Write in complete sentences, too, rather than in note form; although if you find yourself running out of time in an exam, you could use notes to give the reader an idea of the direction your essay was taking (but even here make sure the notes make sense and are not just a list of words).

A systematic approach to writing will help you to make the best use of your time and, hopefully, obviate the need for panic measures. Try to work towards the conclusion which you anticipated in your plan, but there is no problem in modifying your ideas as you write out the essay. The process of examining the subject matter and writing the essay may actually lead you towards a new appraisal of a Joyce text and, accordingly, towards a different conclusion from the one you planned.

By doing this there is a very good chance that what you have written is genuinely your own views about the subject of the essay. This is the whole point of the essay. And it is also the point of this book. I have tried to present what I feel are important topics in Joyce's work and, at the same time, to give my interpretations of his texts. But, more important than this, I set out to show you a *method* by which you can independently tackle Joyce's texts (or anyone else's for that matter) and to form your own interpretations of them. Which is precisely what an essay-question would require.

I suggested above that Joyce's works are sometimes difficult to understand, and yet, at the same time, his works actively invite and accept a wide range of interpretations. In this respect they can be described as open texts. And so I would encourage you to explore them with this point in mind and to use your own, original, insights as the core of your essays on Joyce.

Further reading

Other books by Joyce

Recent years have seen a great increase in the number of editions of Joyce's works. All of his texts are now in print, and as well as his novels and short stories there are his verse and essays, and his only play, details of which are given below.

Exiles (1918: reprinted 1974, by Jonathan Cape), Joyce's only play is, in stage terms, a bit pedestrian, but it presents an interesting version of the eternal triangle and invites comparisons with this aspect of *Ulysses* as well as offering an alternative treatment of Joyce's perennial theme of betrayal. Joyce's own notes, printed in most editions, give some interesting insights into his concept of the artist.

Poems and Shorter Writings (edited by Richard Ellmann, A. Walton Litz and John Whittier-Ferguson; Faber and Faber, 1991) is a very comprehensive collection of Joyce's verse together with occasional pieces and sketches. This edition includes *Giacomo Joyce*, some 'epiphanies' from Joyce's notebooks, and his essay 'A Portrait of the Artist', published in 1904.

The Critical Writings (Faber and Faber, 1959) collects Joyce's essays from 1896 to 1937, from a school essay at age fourteen to a lecture in French on the problems of copyright. This a very useful and enlightening gathering of Joyce's comments on a wide range of topics, on other writers and artists, on Irish politics as well as on his own artistic themes and influences.

Stephen Hero (1944; reprinted 1991, by Jonathan Cape) is the post-humous publication of what remains of Joyce's first version of *A Portrait of the Artist as a Young Man*, after it was supposedly thrown on a fire. It is a straggling, long-winded version of events covered in the final chapter of *A Portrait*, but interesting for the extra light it throws on Stephen's concept of the artist.

Books about Joyce

Since Joyce's death, criticism of his works has passed through a number of more or less distinct phases, corresponding on the whole with changing currents in literary criticism as a whole, and the bibliography below sets out to reflect a range of critical approaches. It will be helpful if I give some idea of these phases.

In the two decades after Joyce's death in 1941, the emphasis in criticism was on explicating themes and references in Joyce's works, and specifically on interpreting them in terms of what was known about his life and his background. Short biographical accounts began to appear soon after his death, usually as reminiscences by close friends, and critics became increasingly interested in the relationship between Joyce and Catholicism. The focus at that time was on *A Portrait* and *Ulysses*, and critics seemed unsure how to respond to the spare and sinewy style of *Dubliners*, while *Finnegans Wake* was generally considered as a literary aberration.

During the 1960s and 1970s, Joyce criticism expanded dramatically, responding to the general rise of literary theory at that time. The literary debate was broadened by the emergence of radical French theories, in particular Marxist and structuralist schools, as well as psychoanalytical approaches. The advent of a more rigorous theoretical basis to criticism allowed critics to engage more fully with the radical nature of Joyce's writing and, in addition, critics began to consider Joyce's individual works within the context of the whole canon of his writing.

The intense concentration on the literariness of a text in these approaches prepared the way for the next critical movement, one which closely examined the relationship between the reader and the text, stressing the independence of the text from its author. In the 1980s and 1990s critics have looked more closely at the role which linguistics can play in a reader's response to the text. This period has seen the arrival of deconstructionist theories, deriving from the ideas of Jacques Derrida, and then of modern psychoanalytical theories, stimulated by the work of Julia Kristeva and Jacques Lacan. In more recent years there has been an increasing interest in feminist and gay interpretations of Joyce's work, as well as attempts to see the work very much in the context of the history of his own time.

Since his death, Joyce's writing has continued to be a very fertile testing ground for literary theory, and the ease with which his work responds to changes in theoretical attitudes is a testimony to the relevance and the richness of its meaning. In the bibliography which follows, I have tried to suggest something of the plurality of the theoretical approaches which have been applied to Joyce. The critical debate continues and Joyce is very much a central figure in that debate.

Inevitably, a critic's interpretation of a text will reflect the background and theoretical interests of that critic, and hence my comments on Joyce in this study are offered only as *some* of the possible interpretations of the works covered here. Naturally you should try to challenge these by working out your own interpretations and by getting other critics' views on Joyce. With this in mind, I would recommend the following books as a good starting point.

1. Biographies

Costello, Peter, *James Joyce: The Years of Growth 1882–1915* (Kyle Cathie, 1992).
(Although limited in its scope, this offers very interesting backgrounds to *Dubliners* and *A Portrait*.)
Ellmann, Richard, *James Joyce* (Oxford University Press, 1982).
(An enormous book with masses of minute detail on every aspect of Joyce's life, art and family.)
Ellmann, Richard, *Selected Letters of James Joyce* (Faber and Faber, 1975).
(Very revealing selection from all stages of Joyce's life.)
Joyce, Stanislaus, *My Brother's Keeper* (Faber and Faber, 1958).
(Readable account of Joyce's early years by his younger brother and benefactor.)

2. The early reception of Joyce's works

Deming, Robert H. (ed.), *James Joyce: The Critical Heritage* (2 vols, Routledge, 1970).

3. General criticism of Joyce

Bolt, Sydney, *A Preface to James Joyce* (Longman, 1981).
(Although its title suggests an introductory study, this is a scholarly and stimulating approach to Joyce.)

Brandabur, Edward, *A Scrupulous Meanness: A Study of Joyce's Early Work* (University of Illinois, 1971).
(A psychoanalytical investigation. A bit wild at times but offers original interpretations.)

Brown, Richard, *James Joyce: A Post-culturalist Perspective* (Macmillan, 1992).
(Introduces Joyce's work in its historical context.)

Levin, Harry, *James Joyce: A Critical Introduction* (Faber and Faber, 1941).
(An early overview of Joyce's work but still an excellent introduction.)

Parrinder, Patrick, *James Joyce* (Cambridge University Press, 1984).
(An exceptionally stimulating study of the whole Joyce canon.)

Pierce, David, *James Joyce's Ireland* (Yale University, 1992).
(Very readable survey of the Irish elements in the work, plus photographs.)

Tindall, William York, *A Reader's Guide to James Joyce* (Thames and Hudson, 1960).
(Strong on detail, especially the Irish background.)

Wales, Katie, *The Language of James Joyce* (Macmillan, 1992).
(Joyce's particular use of language, especially good on *Dubliners* and *Ulysses*)

4. Collections of essays on Joyce

Attridge, Derek (ed.), *The Cambridge Companion to James Joyce* (Cambridge University Press, 1990).
(A very thorough reference work written by Joyce scholars.)

Beja, Maurice (ed.), *James Joyce: 'Dubliners' and 'A Portrait of the Artist as a Young Man'* (Macmillan, 1973).
(Gathers together interesting background material on these two works plus some important critical essays.)

Chace, William M. (ed.), *Joyce: A Collection of Critical Essays* (Prentice Hall, 1974).
(Many important early essays.)

Henke, Suzette and Elaine Unkeless (eds), *Women in Joyce* (Harvester Press, 1982).
(Views on each of Joyce's works and his treatment of female characters.)
McCabe, Colin (ed.), *James Joyce: New Perspectives* (Macmillan, 1982).
(Offers more advanced analyses, applying contemporary literary theory.)

5. Books on individual works

Dubliners

Gifford, Don, *Joyce Annotated: Notes for 'Dubliners' and 'A Portrait of the Artist as a Young Man'* (University of California, 1982).
Hart, Clive (ed.), *James Joyce's 'Dubliners': Critical Essays* (Faber and Faber, 1969).
Torchiana, Donald T., *Backgrounds for James Joyce's 'Dubliners'* (Allen and Unwin, 1984).

A Portrait of the Artist as a Young Man

Blades, John, *James Joyce: 'A Portrait of the Artist as a Young Man'* (Penguin, 1991).
Gifford, Don, (see above, under *Dubliners*).
Seed, David, *James Joyce's 'A Portrait of the Artist as a Young Man'* (Harvester, 1992).

Ulysses

Ellmann, Richard, *'Ulysses' on the Liffey* (Faber and Faber, 1974).
Gifford, Don, *'Ulysses' Annotated: Notes for James Joyce's 'Ulysses'* (University of California, 1989).
Groden, Michael, *'Ulysses' in Progress* (Princeton University, 1977).
Hart, Clive and David Hayman (eds), *James Joyce's 'Ulysses': Critical Essays* (University of California, 1974).
Kenner, Hugh, *Ulysses* (John Hopkins University, 1982).
Lawrence, Karen, *The Odyssey of Style in 'Ulysses'* (Princeton University, 1981).

Finnegans Wake

Atherton, James S., *The Books at the Wake* (Faber and Faber, 1959).
Gordon, John, *'Finnegans Wake': A Plot Summary* (Syracuse University, 1986).
Hayman, David, *The 'Wake' in Transit* (Cornell University, 1990).
McHugh, Roland, *Annotations to 'Finnegans Wake'* (Routledge, 1980).
McHugh, Roland, *The 'Finnegans Wake' Experience* (Irish Academic Press, 1981).
Tindall, William York, *A Reader's Guide to 'Finnegans Wake'* (Thames and Hudson, 1969).